IPAD 10TH GENERATION USER GUIDE

Complete Manual for Seniors & Beginners on How to Master the New 10.9" iPad with Step By Step Pictures & Illustrations | Tips & Tricks For iPadOS 16

Henry K Mills

CONTENTS

INTRODUCTION

Welcome to the world of iPads. Over here we are activity oriented. If you've bought one of the iPad 10th generation, congrats and welcome to the pack! If you've not, then don't delay. Congrats also for getting this book.

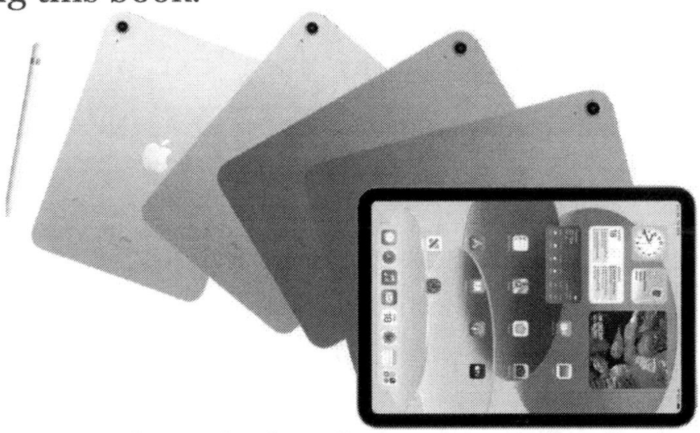

This personal guide has been specially designed to help walk you through your journey in setting up and using your new iPad. You are going to find it handy as you go on, so don't be quick to discard it. If possible, keep it among your documents, safe and secure.

The new iPad 10 is packed with amazing variety of colors. Its enhanced camera creates a better video conferencing experience than older models. This amazing device creates the perfect environment for content creators, students and gamers. It will absolutely boost your productivity, creativity and self-expression, you can be sure of that. You can create cinematic home videos with it, play games, draw beautiful realistic art works, develop apps, and on and on.

In this book you're going to be learning all the basic things you need to use your iPad comfortably. There are twenty six chapters you'll be coming across, each of which discusses a particular aspect of the iPad. Have you been using the new camera features in FaceTime? Look out for pro tips to boost your video conferencing skills with FaceTime and make your calls more professional. There are countless pictures to ease the learning process and basic terms you need to know have been explained.

The first few chapters deal with getting used to your iPad, its parts, basic accessories, how to charge it and how to set it up, including connecting to a Wi-Fi network.

Chapters 6 to 10 cover Settings and features of the operating system of your iPad, some of which include installing Siri the iPad voice assistant, using the virtual keyboard, browsing the internet with Safari, setting your wallpaper and ringtones, notifications and finally, how to synchronize your iPad with your other devices.

The remaining chapters deal on applications (popularly called apps) that run on your iPad, such as reminder, Facetime, Camera, iMessage, Calendar, Mail, Sidecar, Scribble, Notes, etc.

Check out others in the Series

If you love Apple products, you'll definitely love the Series, '**Apple Devices By Funky Traders**'. It discusses how to comfortably use various Apple devices like iPhones, Macbooks, iPads, Apple Watches, and many more. Check these amazing books out.

To begin, bring out your iPad, and let's take a look at some of the features of this device.

CHAPTER 1: GETTING TO KNOW THE IPAD

Now that you have the iPad, the next step is to learn about the physical features of your device and the accessories that come with it. We'll describe some important buttons and ports, how to switch on your device and turn it off, charging the battery, and important tips about protecting your IPad's screen.

Parts of the iPad

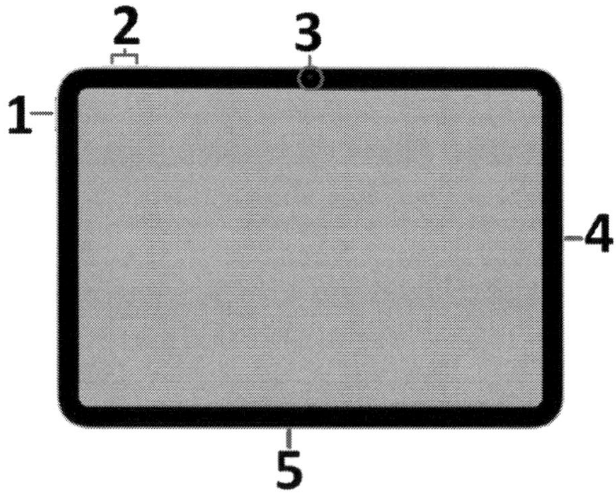

Fig 1- Parts of the iPad

1. *Top button*
2. *Volume buttons*
3. *Selfie/front camera*
4. *USB-C Ports*
5. *Magnetic Connector*

- **Buttons:** The iPad has three important buttons, the Top button and two volume buttons.

The top button is used for touch ID, for turning off your ipad and for locking and unlocking it. The volume buttons are used for increasing and decreasing the volume of your iPad.

- **Cameras:** There are two cameras; one Front camera for video calls and selfies and two rear cameras for snapping photos of others and for scanning of documents.
- **Smart Connector:** This side of the iPad is used for joining the iPad to an Apple Smart Keyboard.
- **USB-C Ports:** These are holes through which you're going to connect the iPad to a source of power if you want to charge it or to a computer or Camera if you want to transfer files or pictures. You're going to insert one end of the USB-C cord into this point.

In The Box

iPad currently comes with the following accessories:

Lightning-USB cable: For connecting to a computer and an AC adapter.

USB power adapter: For charging the battery. The size and type of adapter depends on the country or region. You can also use the charging cable to connect your iPad to your computer to download, transfer files, use your iPad as a second screen on your Mac, and more.

A picture of these two is shown below.

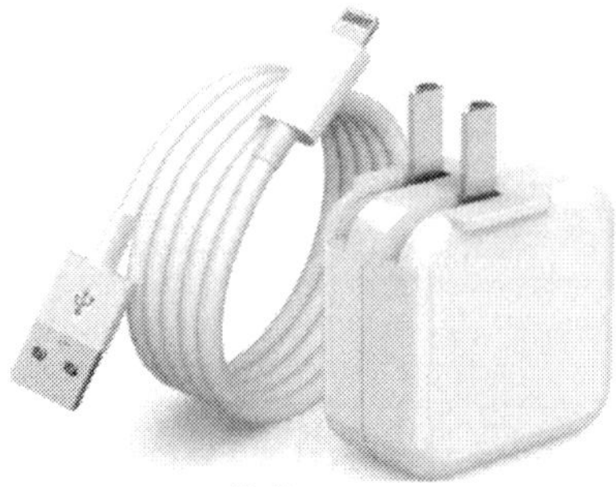

Fig 2- USB C cable & Power Adapter

CHAPTER 2: SETTING UP

When you turn on your iPad for the first time, you will be asked to select some settings like selected language, Wi-Fi network, Apple ID and more. You don't have to answer all these many questions when you are setting up. You can skip some of them now and change them later.

After opening the iPad from its box, click and hold the power button to turn it on. Wait for the operating system (OS) to finish booting, and then follow these steps:

1. Please select the language of the operating system. Most third-party applications you install will also reflect this language setting.

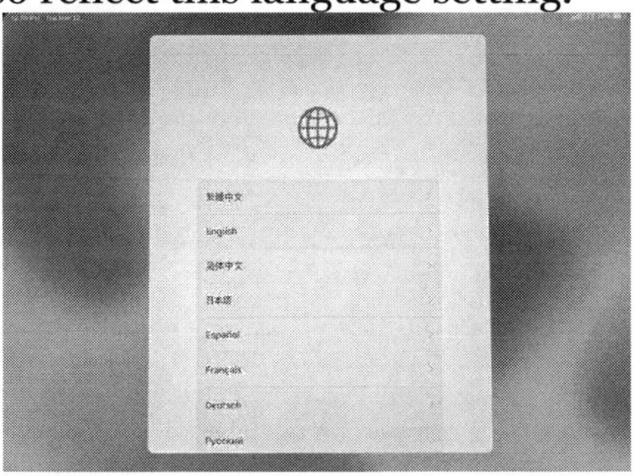

Fig 3- Select the language

2. Please select your region or country. This will adjust the service and features accordingly.

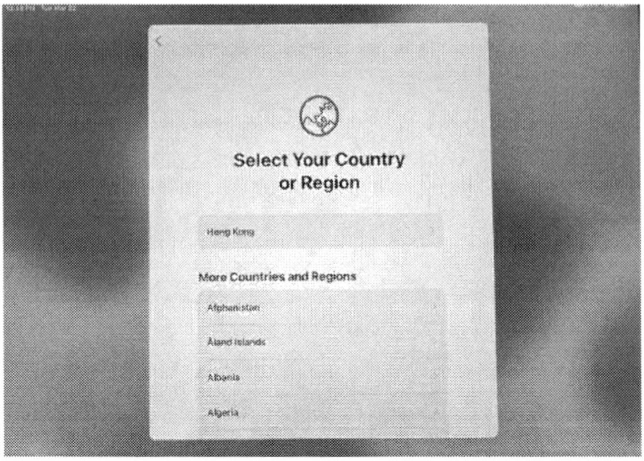

Fig 4- Select your region

3. If you have another Device operating iOS / iPad operating system, you can move it closer to the new iPad to transfer data quickly. Otherwise, press **Set Up Manually** to start from scratch.

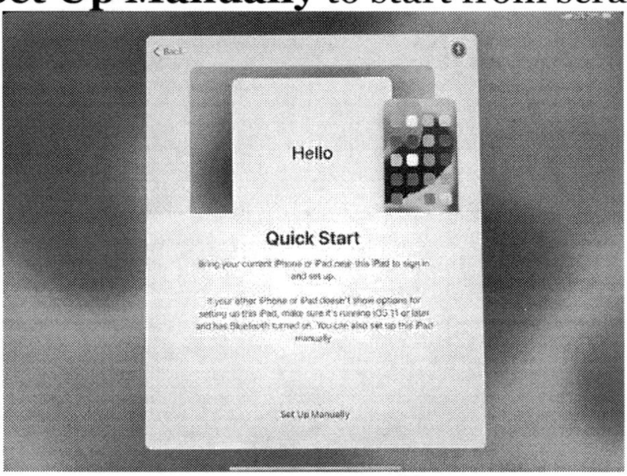

Fig 5- Press Set Up Manually to start from scratch

4. Please check your language setting. You can make all the necessary changes by clicking on **Customize settings**.

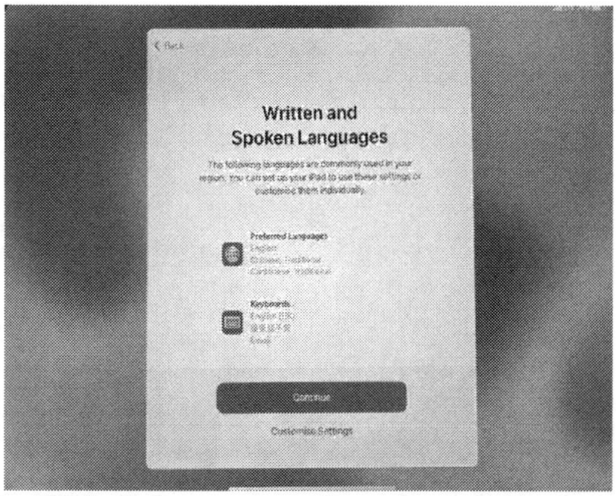

Fig 6- Clicking on Customize settings

5. The Preferred Language setting allows you to select the priority of the spoken language. For example, if your app does not support English, it is by default a traditional Chinese language.

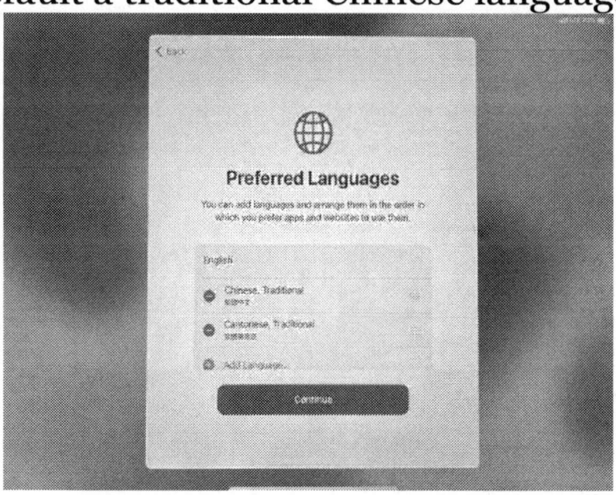

Fig 7- Pick Preferred Language

6. Select the language you want to add to your iPad keyboard and click **Continue**.

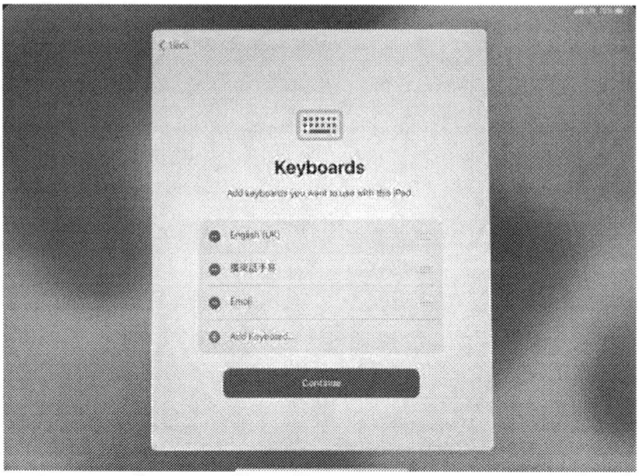

Fig 8- Select the language and click Continue

7. Dictating allows you to turn your speech into text. Select the language you use in Dictation and click **Continue**.

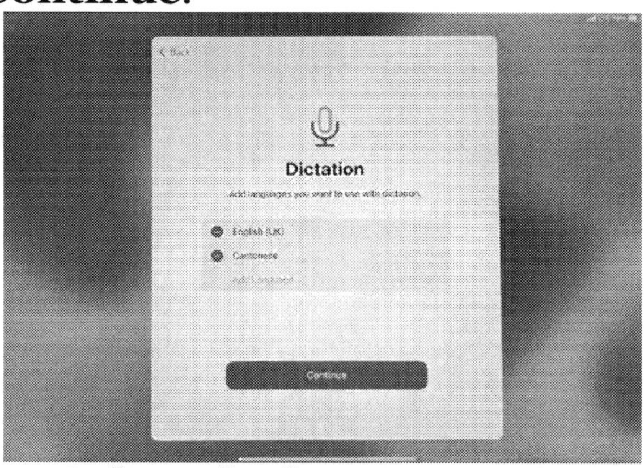

Fig 9- Select the language you use in Dictation

8. Click on your name and enter your password to connect to your Wi-Fi home network. An Internet connection is required to complete the installation process and take advantage of the features that come with the iPad OS.

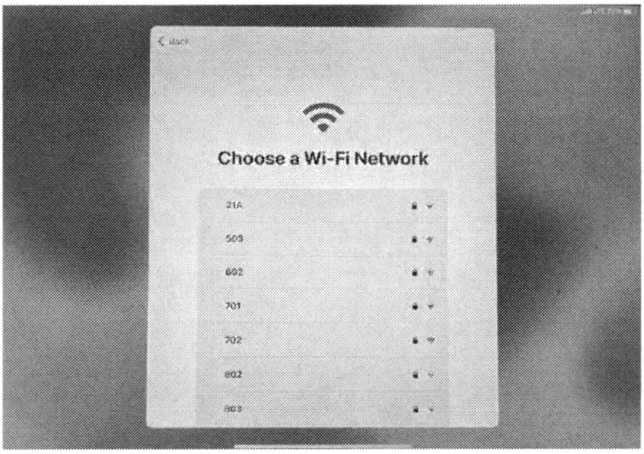

Fig 10- Connect to your Wi-Fi home network

9. It can take up to a few minutes for your iPad to connect and activate your Apple server. This is to make sure you have not been robbed and start counting down the warranty that comes with it.

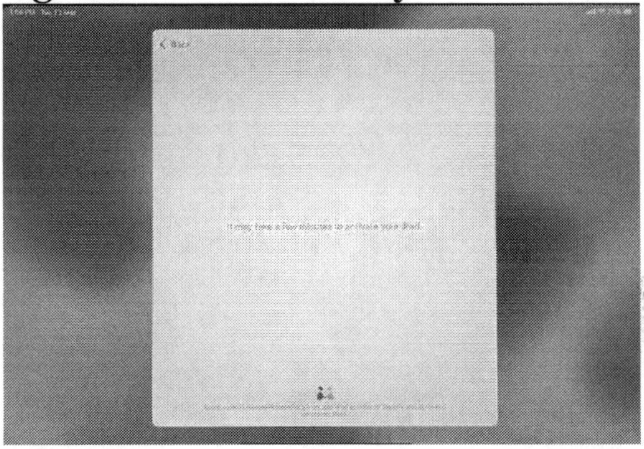

Fig 11- Connect and activate your Apple server

10. Carefully read Apple's data and privacy policy and click **Continue**.
11. Set **Touch ID** as an option. This allows you to unlock the iPad by placing your finger on the power button.

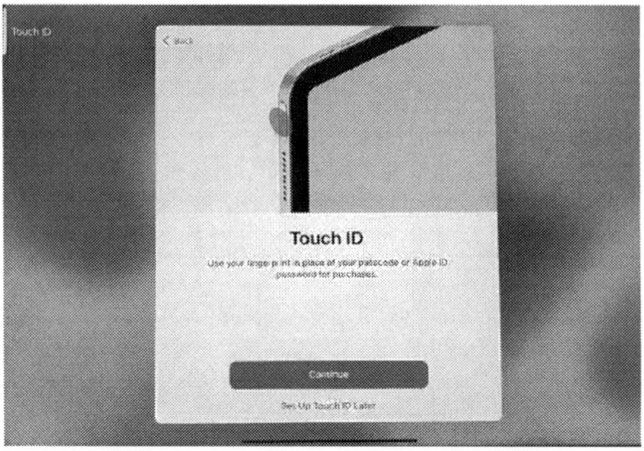

Fig 12- Set Touch ID

12. To set the Touch ID, release the switch repeatedly with your finger to record your fingerprint.
13. After setting up Touch ID, you need to select a password as a security measure. You can change your passcode from a numeric passcode to an alphanumeric password using the **Password Options** button. Once you have determined the type of password, enter it twice to confirm it.

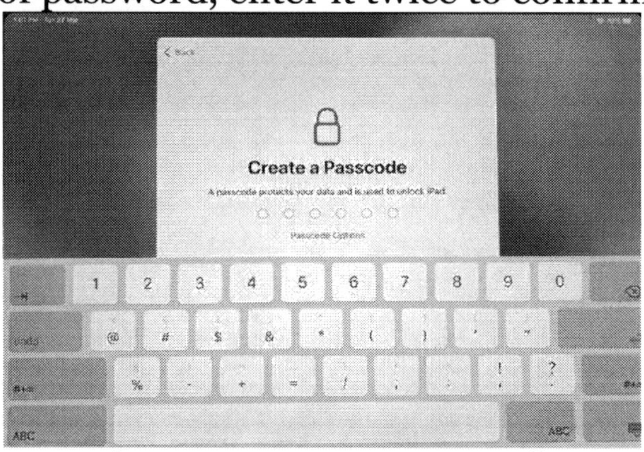

Fig 13- Create Passcode

14. Next, **Apps & Data**: Decide whether to restore your Cloud or local backup from another device. Alternatively, you can click Do not transfer applications and data to start from scratch.

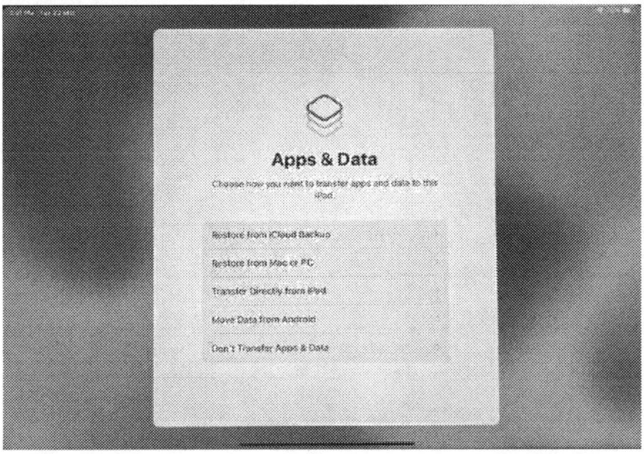

Fig 14- Transfer Apps & Data

15. Sign in to your Apple ID to access company features like iMessage, FaceTime and App Store downloads.

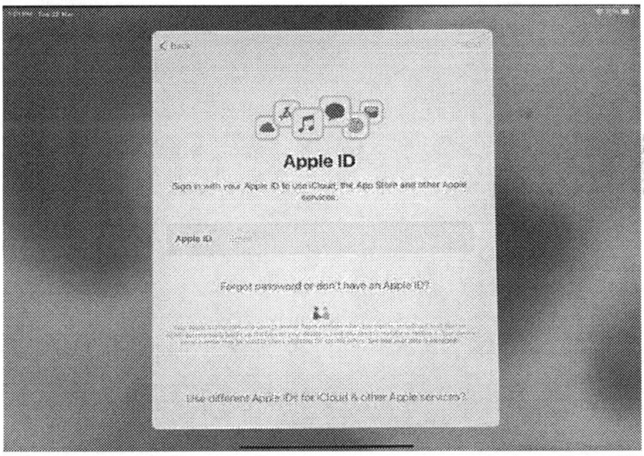

Fig 15- Sign in to your Apple ID

16. Please read the Terms of Use carefully and click [**Agree**] if you agree. If you do not agree, you will not be able to use the new iPad.

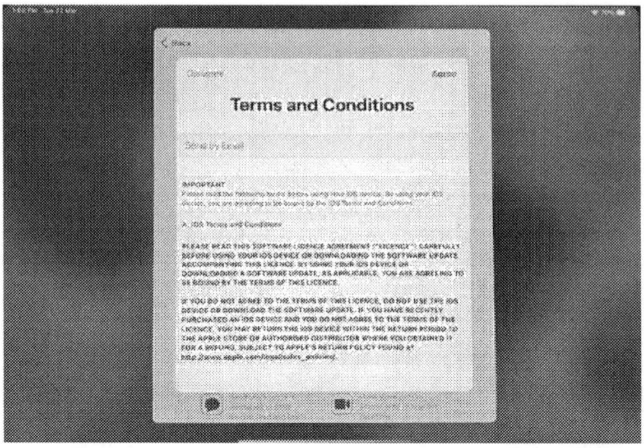

Fig 16- Agree to Terms & Conditions

17. Click **Continue** to get automatic iPad OS software updates in the future. You can disable this option later in normal settings.

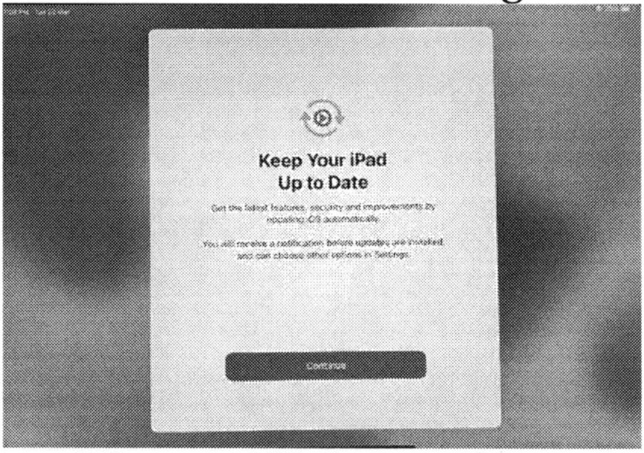

Fig 17- Click Continue

18. If necessary, enable Location Services to help your app provide more accurate information and use navigation services and maps.

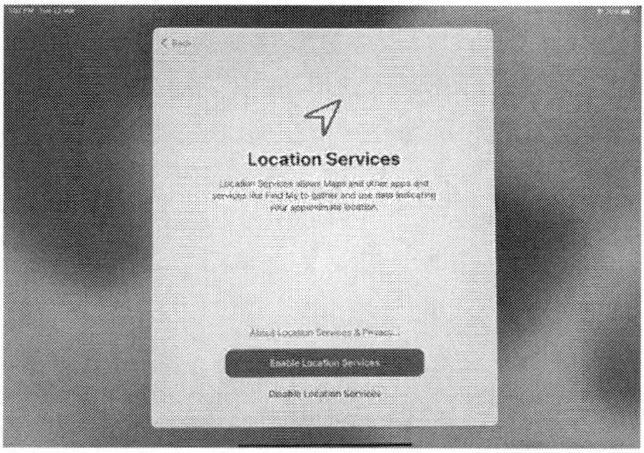

Fig 18- Enable Location Services

19. If you like, you can enable Siri, a virtual assistant. Siri can answer your questions, perform tasks and provide relevant information in a timely manner.

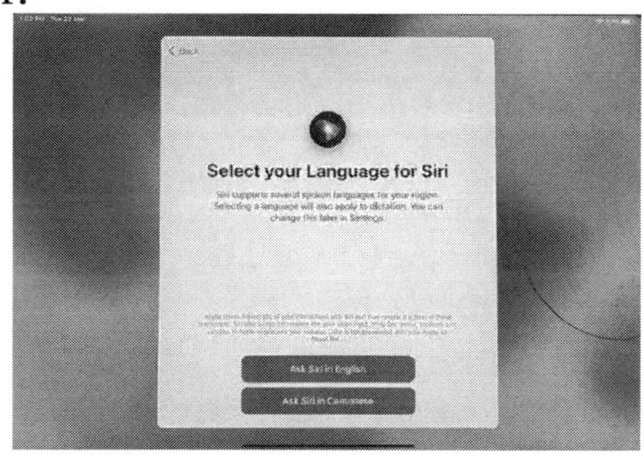

Fig 19- Enable Siri

20. If you enable Siri, decide which language you want Siri to use.

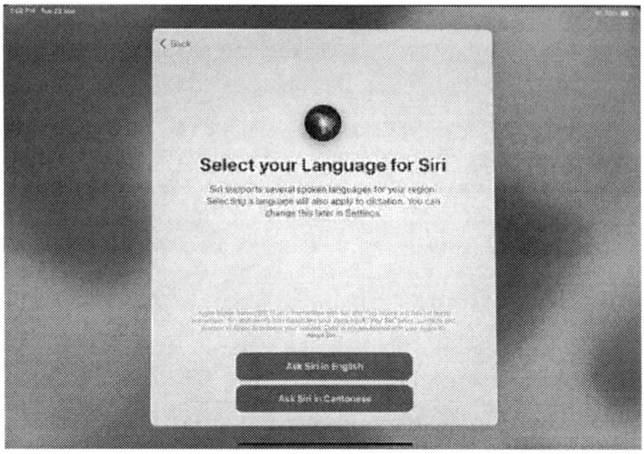

Fig 20- Pick Siri Language

21. Select the sound you want to use with Siri. The included voice has different emphases and human characteristics, so you can choose the voice that suits you.

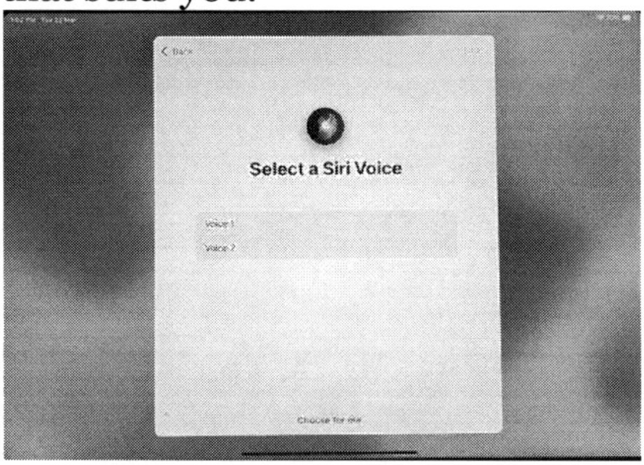

Fig 21- Pick Siri Voice

22. Activate Hey Siri if necessary. This allows you to call Siri hands-free by saying Hey Siri.

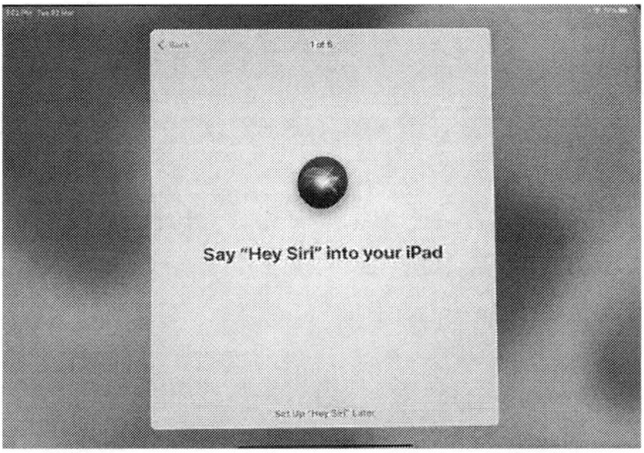

Fig 22- Activate Hey Siri

23. Choose whether Apple should collect audio recordings to improve Siri. If you decide to share them, your data will be anonymous and will not be linked to your credentials.
24. Screen time monitors the time spent on iPad and sets optional limits and child supervision. You can optionally click Continue to enable this feature.

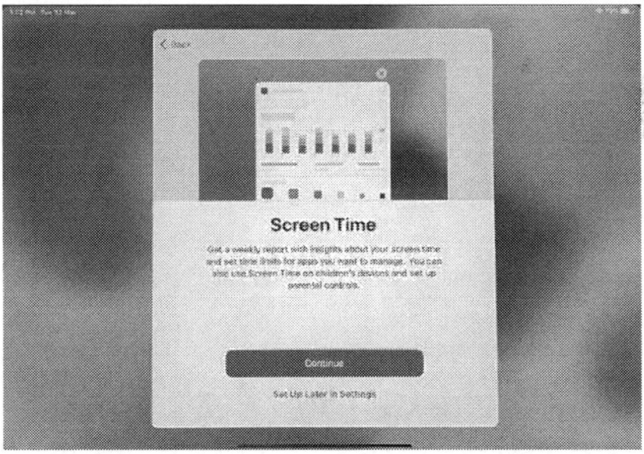

Fig 23- Set Screen time or Continue

25. Apple collects anonymous logs from your iPad and which it uses to improve its products and services. Blocking or allowing this is optional.
26. Decide if you want to use your iPad in light or dark mode. You can later select the automatic option in the display settings. Dark mode adds a gray / black background to the system and supported apps and light mode make it a lighter color like white.

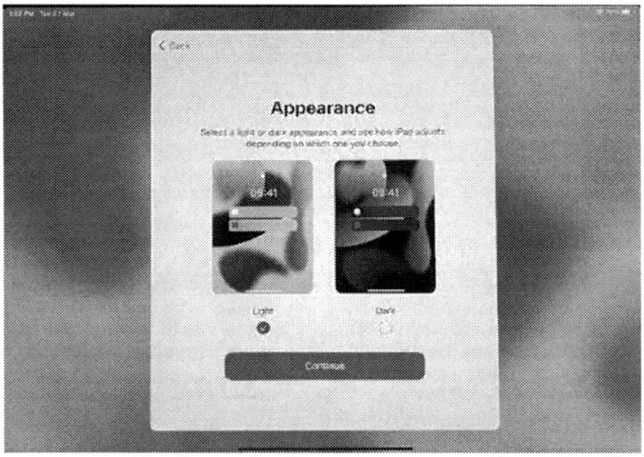

Fig 24- Pick Light or Dark mode

27. Click Getting Started to get started with iPad.

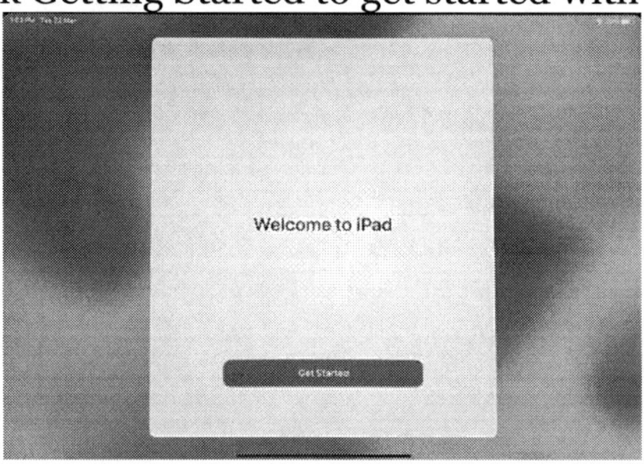

Fig 25- Get Started

28. Congratulations!

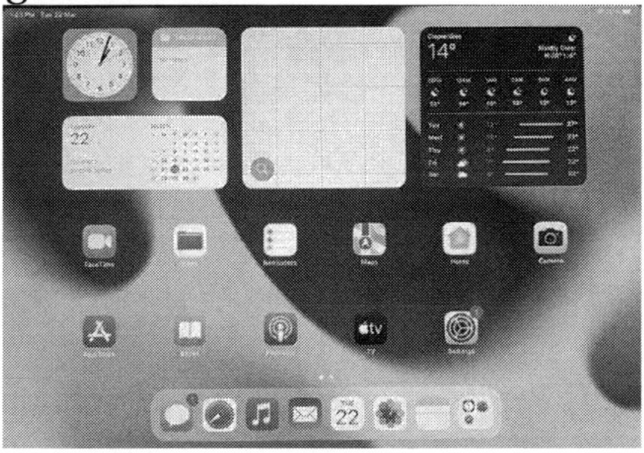

Fig 26- Home screen

CHAPTER 3: BEGINNER'S TIPS

To put your iPad to sleep and wake it up

When you are ready to use the iPad, you need to wake it up by pressing the top button. The lock screen appears.
From here, you have two options for unlocking your iPad.

Password: You can unlock your iPad using the numeric password you selected when you first set up iPad. Just press the top button again and enter your password.

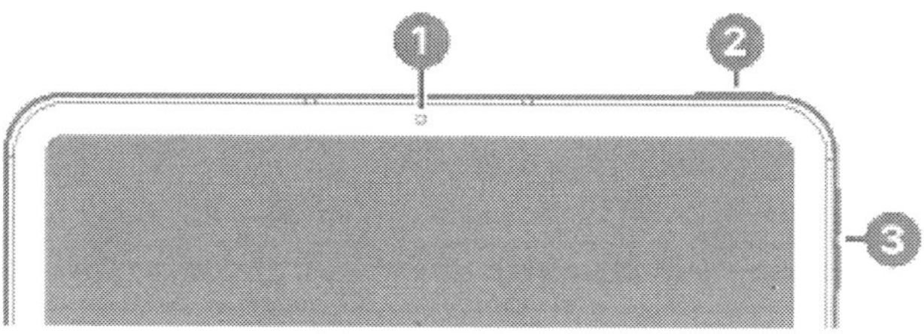

1. *Selfie Camera*
2. *Top button*
3. *Volume buttons*

Touch ID: This scans your fingerprint to unlock your iPad. After waking up the iPad, simply place your finger or thumb on the top button to unlock the iPad. For more information on installing and using Touch ID, see the chapter on iPad Security and General Settings.

After using the iPad, press the top button to put it into sleep mode. This will turn off the screen and extend the battery life. If you do not use the iPad for more than a few minutes, the iPad automatically enters sleep mode.

To turn iPad on and off:

Most often, you will not need to put off your iPad. You can simply put it to sleep mode using the top button. However, some other times, you're going to have to turn it off completely (like when you are in an airplane). Do this:

Turn off the iPad: Hold down the top button and one of the volume keys at the same time, and then drag the slider.

Turn on your iPad: Hold the button at the top until you see the Apple logo.

Charge your iPad battery

The device lasts for about 10 hours during normal use. When it is low it needs to be charged.

You will find the battery icon in the upper right edge of your iPad screen. It shows the battery level and whether it is charging. Lightning battery symbol indicates that the battery is charging.

If you are syncing or using an iPad, it may take some time to charge the battery.

There are two ways to charge the battery.

- Connect your iPad to an electrical outlet with the included cable and power adapter.

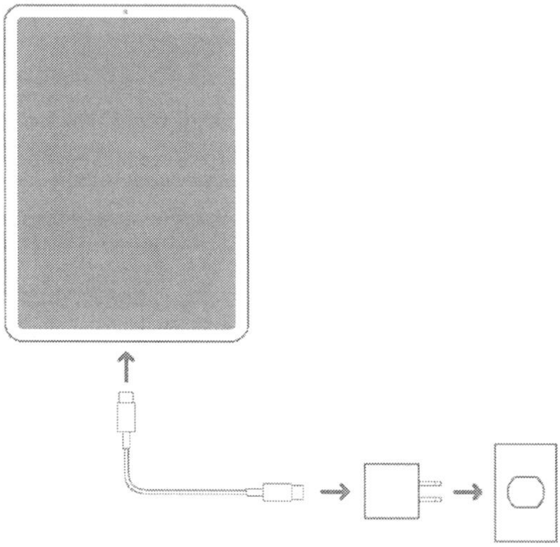

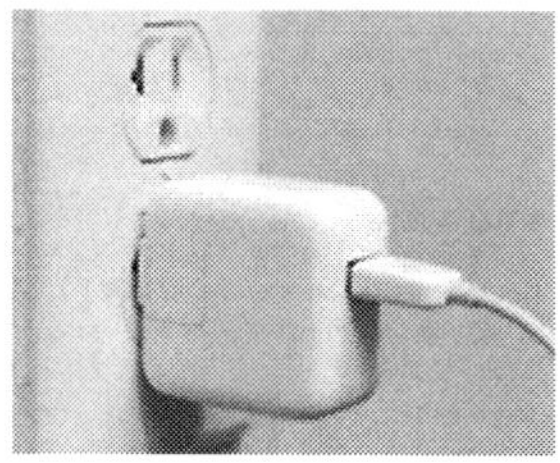

Or

- Using a USB-C cord, connect the iPad with a computer.
- Make sure your computer is turned on. If your iPad is connected to a computer that is turned off, it may drain the battery instead of charging it. Look for the charging icon in the battery icon to make sure your iPad is being charged.
- If your Mac or PC does not have enough power to charge your iPad, the status bar will display the message "Not charging".

Note: Do not connect the iPad to the keyboard and try charging it.

Caring for and protecting your iPad

To properly care for and protect your iPad, you are going to need other accessories such as iPad cases and covers (sold separately). If you do not have one yet then it is time to find one that suits your style, budget and personal needs.

There are various options available in the Apple Store, including the popular Smart Cover. The Smart Cover is designed specifically for the iPad and can also be used as a stand.

If you're not interested in the Smart Cover (or any of the Apple Store cases), do not worry. Search online or in retail stores and you will find hundreds of options. No matter what you choose, good holsters and covers will help protect your device so much that you can enjoy it for years to come.

You're also going to need a soft, lint-free cloth to wipe fingerprints and dirt off the screen of your iPad. Never use household cleaners, alcohol or other abrasives.

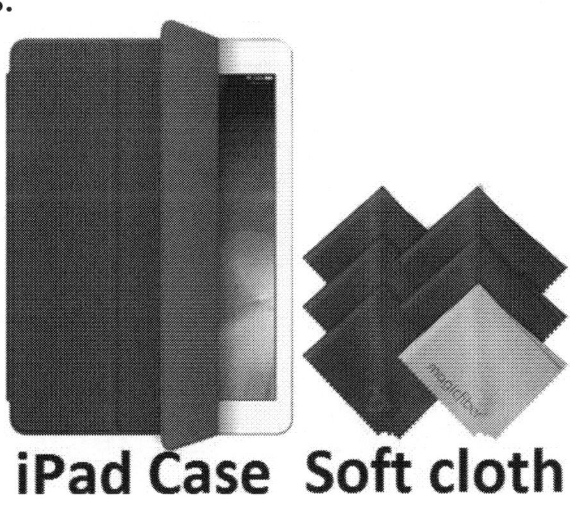

Recommended Accessories

Apple Pencil: There are also some accessories you can buy, such as the apple pencil (2nd generation). It's used for drawing, taking notes, and making marks on pictures and screenshots.
Magic Keyboard: This is a wireless keyboard you can use with your iPad to make typing faster.

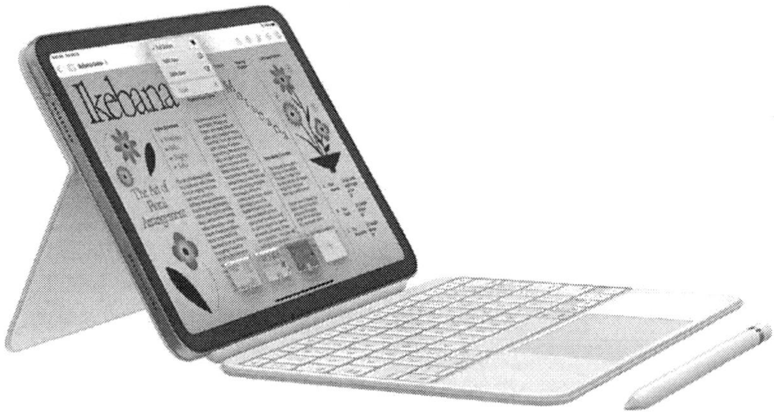

Apple Pencil & Magic Keyboard

CHAPTER 4: USING IPADOS

To use iPad, you need to understand the basics of iPadOS, the iPad operating system. iPadOS Appears the first time you turn on your iPad. iPadOS enhances the iPad's practical capabilities, including a multi-touch screen, easy-to-use interface and built-in apps. In short, this is what makes the iPad function the way it does.

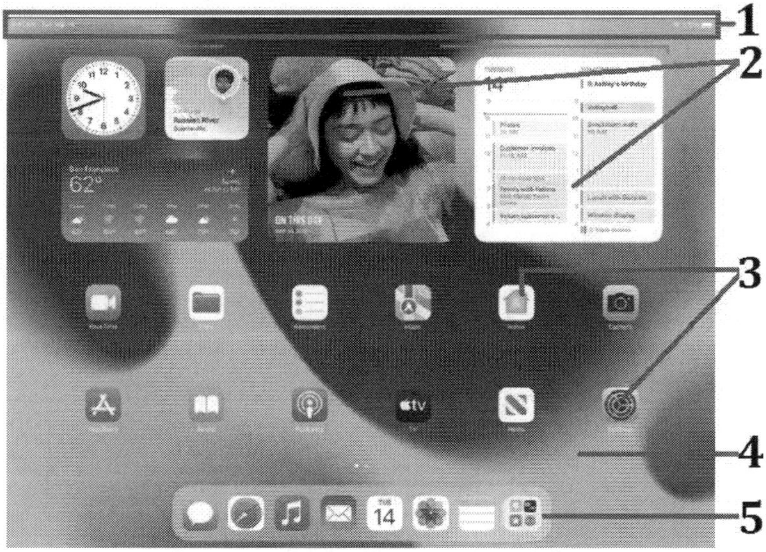

Fig 27: iPadOS Interface

1. *Status bar*
2. *Widgets*
3. *App icons*
4. *Home Screen*
5. *Dock*

What makes up the iPadOS interface

Status bar

The status bar at the top of the screen shows current information about your iPad. This includes the status of your internet connection, time and battery level.

Apps

The icon/symbol that appears here is a shortcut to the app. In this example, the icon represents some of the built-in apps that come with iPadOS. If you choose to download more applications, the icon will also appear here. To open an application, just click on the application you want.

Home screen

The screen that appears here is called the home screen. However, to help you understand it, think of it as the equivalent of the desktop of a computer. All applications are saved here and only appear when you switch on your device. You can also use multiple home screens to free up space for more applications and organize your icons. To move between screens, swipe left or right.

Dock

The dock at the bottom of the screen is designed for the apps you use most often. It usually contains five apps including Mail, Photos, Music, Files and Safari. You can change the contents of the Dock by inserting or removing icons. This way you will always find your favorite apps.

Multi-touch Gestures

Gestures, sometimes called multi-touch gestures, are used to open apps and browse the web.

Simple gestures:

Tap, touch and hold, swipe, scroll, zoom.

- **Tap**. Touch lightly with one finger on the screen.
- **Press and hold.** Press and hold an item in the application to preview the content in response. From the Home screen, briefly press and hold the application icon to open the shortcut menu.
- **Swipe** Move one finger quickly on the screen.
- **Scroll**. Move one finger on the screen without lifting. For example, in the photos app, you can scroll through a list, dragging up or down to see more pictures. Swipe to scroll quickly. To stop scrolling, touch the screen.
- **Zoom.** Place two fingers close to each other on the screen. Spread them out and enlarge, or bring them closer together and zoom out.
  You can also double-tap an image or webpage to enlarge, or tap twice again for further zooming.
  On the map app, double-click, hold and drag up to zoom in, or drag down to zoom out.

Advanced Gestures

Go home. You can return to the home screen at any time by swiping from the bottom of the screen.

Fig 28. Go Home: Swipe up

Quickly open Controls: Swipe down from the upper right edge of the screen to access the control panel. If you'd like to see more options, hold the control. See Using and Customizing the Control Panel on the iPad.

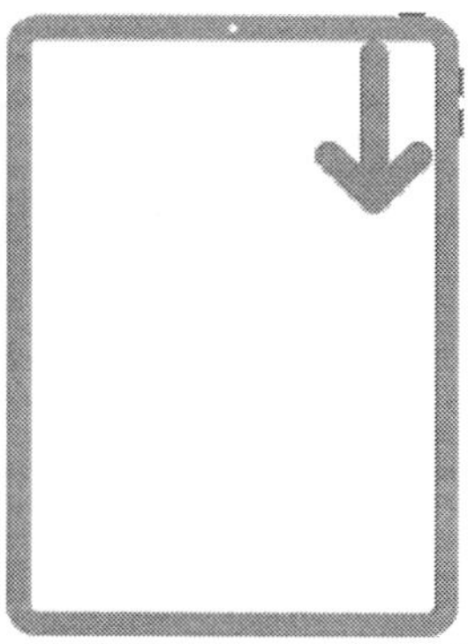

Fig 29. Open Control Center: Swipe down from the upper right edge of the screen

Open the application switcher. Swipe up from the bottom edge, pause when you get to the center of the screen, and then lift your finger. To look through open applications, swipe right, and then tap the application you want to use. See Switch apps on iPad.

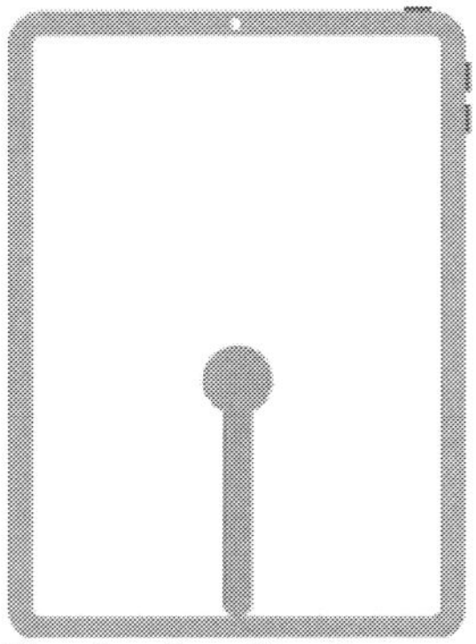

Fig 30. Open App Switch: Swipe up from the bottom edge, pause when you get to the center of the screen, and then lift your finger.

Switch between open applications. Swipe left or right along the bottom edge of the screen to quickly switch between open applications. See switch between iPad applications.

Fig 31. Switch between open applications

Open the Dock while inside an app. Swipe up from the bottom edge of the screen to pause and highlight Dock. To open another application quickly, click on the app in the Dock.

Fig 32. Open the Dock while inside an app

Take a screenshot. Press and release the top button and one of the volume keys at the same time.

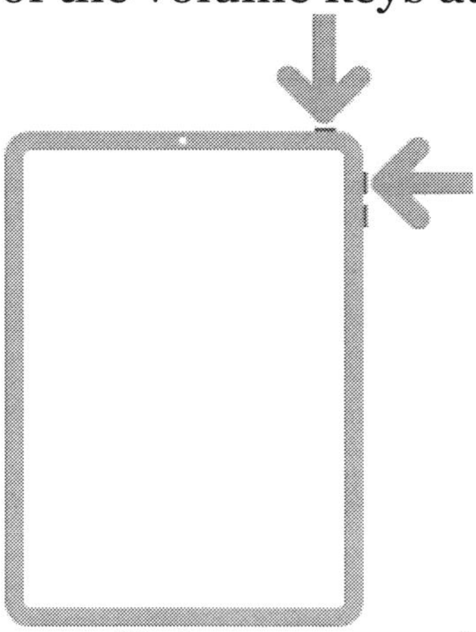

Fig 33. Take a screenshot

Switch off. Hold down the top button and one of the volume keys at the same time until you see the slider, then drag the top slider to turn it off.

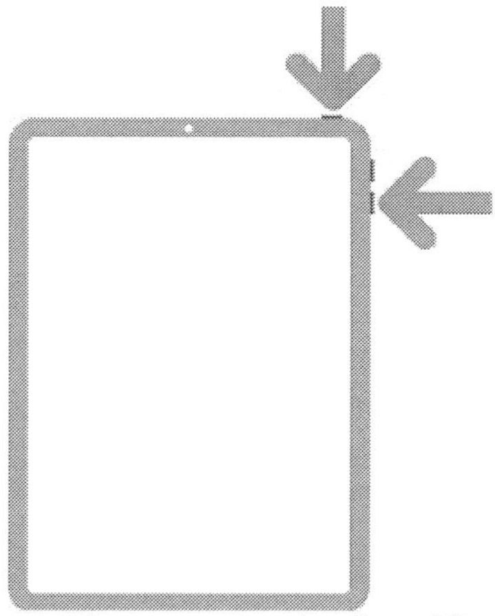

Fig 34. Switch off

Force restart. Press and hold the volume key next to the top button, press and release the other volume key quickly, and press and hold the top key until you see the Apple logo. Three steps, a little tricky, but once you master it, it becomes easy.

Understand the app

Even if you are using the iPad for the first time, you likely must have heard of applications (app for short) before. The idea is simple. An application is a computer program designed to run on your iPad.

The iPad comes with several built-in apps that you can access directly from your home screen. It's a great place for new users to get started, as nothing needs to be downloaded or installed. Many of these applications are out of the box (like the camera application) and ready to use, but other applications (such as email and contacts) require a little more installation. Later in this book, we will look at some of the built-in applications.

After reviewing the apps that came with your device, try downloading more from the App Store. There are thousands of applications that you can download for free. Many other programs cost only $0.99, but some are more expensive.

iPadOS features

Now that you understand the basics of using iOS, it's a good idea to get acquainted with some of the useful features of iOS. You can access these features at any time, regardless of the application you are using.

Notifications

Notifications are pop-ups, banners, and other audio and video signals that work with applications on your device. This is designed to let you know when something needs attention or when there is recent activity (Facebook, Tiktok, telegrams, email, etc.).

Notifications behave differently depending on the application, but they all have one thing in common. It helps you keep up with your daily tasks and responsibilities. Notifications come:

- As a warning/alert (popup or banner)
- As a signal/badge on the application's icon itself
- Through Notification Center (you can always open it by swiping down, away from the status bar)

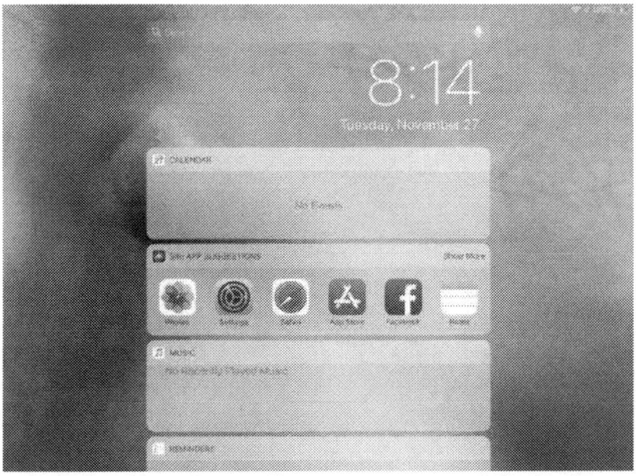

Fig 35. iPad Lock Screen Notifications

Control center

The control panel gives you quick access to settings that are often used on your device and game boards with playback controls. Simply swipe down from the top right corner of the home screen to access the control panel.

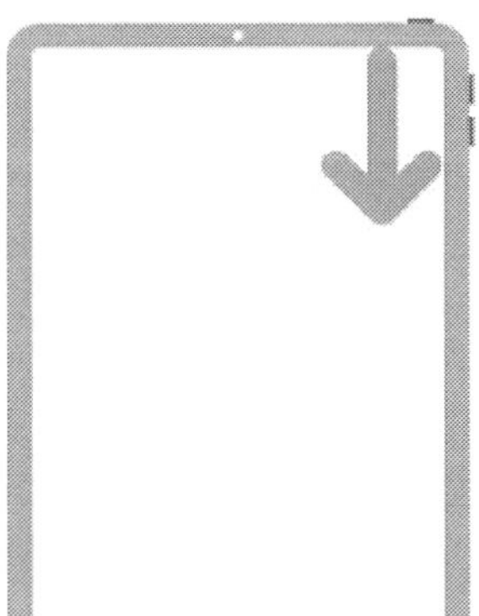

Fig 36. Open Control Center

What makes up the Control Center?

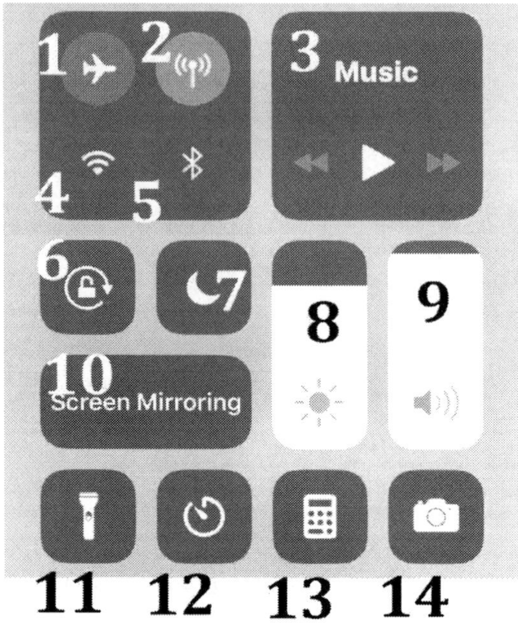

Fig 37. Control Center items

1. *Airplane Mode*
2. *Mobile Data*
3. *Music controls*
4. *WiFi*
5. *Bluetooth*
6. *Portrait orientation lock*
7. *Don't Disturb*
8. *Brightness*
9. *Volume*
10. *Screen Mirroring*
11. *Flash light*
12. *Clock*
13. *Calculator*
14. *Camera*

- **Flight/Airplane Mode**

Enabling this option activates Airplane mode and turns off Wi-Fi and 3G / 4G/5G.

- **Mobile Data**

Change these options to turn Mobile Data on and off. This allows you to browse the internet, share photos, locations, etc. with other Apple devices nearby, use apps like Apple Music, App Store etc.

- **WiFi**

Turn on this option to turn the Wi-Fi connection on and off.

- **Blue tooth**

Change these options to turn the Bluetooth connection on and off.

- **Portrait mode lock**

Activate this option to turn the face lock on and off. This prevents the screen from rotating when you switch on the device.

- **Do not disturb**

Change these options to use silent mode. This silences calls and notifications while the phone is locked.

- **Brightness**

Use this option to adjust the brightness of the iPad screen.

- **Volume**

Use this option to adjust the volume on your iPad.

- **Screen Mirroring**

Tap this to connect your iPad to an Apple TV and cast your iPad's screen to that TV.

- **Mute**

Press this button to turn off or turn off the iPad's sounds quickly.

- **Timer**

  Press the timer button to open the timer application.

- **Calculator**

Tap the Calculator button to open the Calculator app.

- **Camera**

Tap the camera button to open the camera application.

Siri

Siri is a useful feature that comes with the latest versions of the iPad. Sometimes called a virtual assistant, he can help you with all sorts of things. For instance, you can use Siri to send messages, schedule appointments, and search for nearby restaurants. Controlled by the sound of your voice, not the gestures or keyboard, it can follow along with and respond to day to day commands like, 'remind me that I have an appointment with the doctor on the 18th', 'How is the weather today?'

CHAPTER 5: WI-FI

You need to connect your iPad to the Internet to use most features. It's easy to go online by turning your iPad's wireless connection on or off, or connecting to a nearby network. When you connect to the network, your device automatically connects to the network at any time within reach. If you do not have a network within reach, connect with 3G or 4G instead, but only if you have a 3G or 4G-enabled device (and a contract with a wireless service provider).

To turn Wi-Fi on or off:

Turn on your iPad. The first page that appears is called the home screen.

- From this screen, press on the settings icon 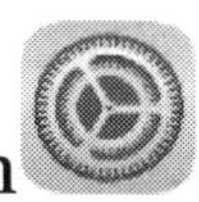 .
- The settings are displayed. Tap Wi-Fi in the left pane.
- Next to Wi-Fi, tap the control to turn it on (green) or off.

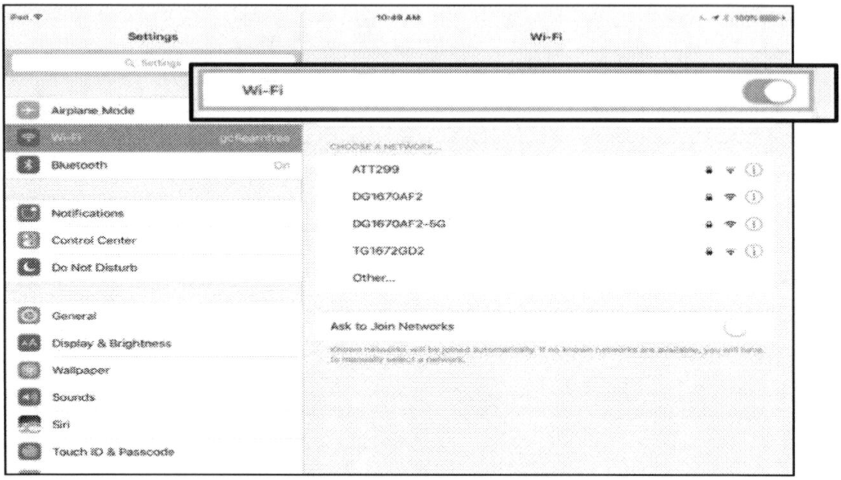

Connect to a Network

To connect to a network within easy reach (for example, Wi-Fi in your home or a public hotspot nearby), search for the network in 'Choose a network'. Now press a network you'll be using. If your network is secure, you will need to enter your password to connect to the network.

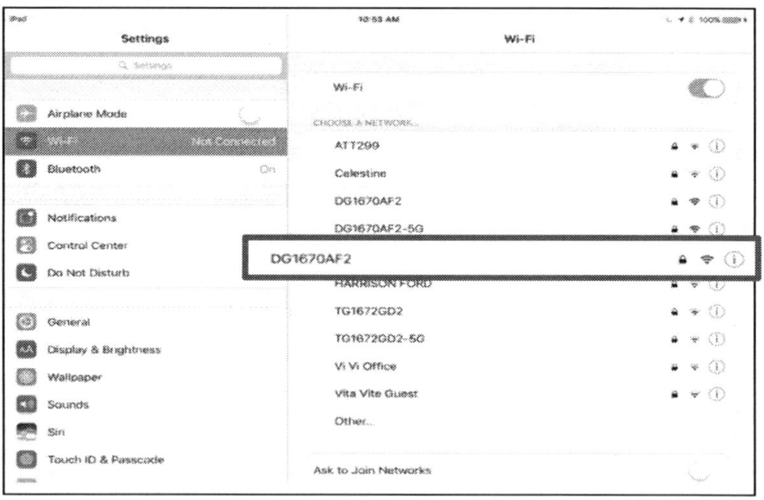

If your network is insecure, you can connect without a password, but be cautious when connecting to a an insecure network (especially for public networks such as Wi-Fi on local cafes). What you see or share over an insecure network can easily be seen by others who are using that same network (for example, a thief can easily hack into your email account).

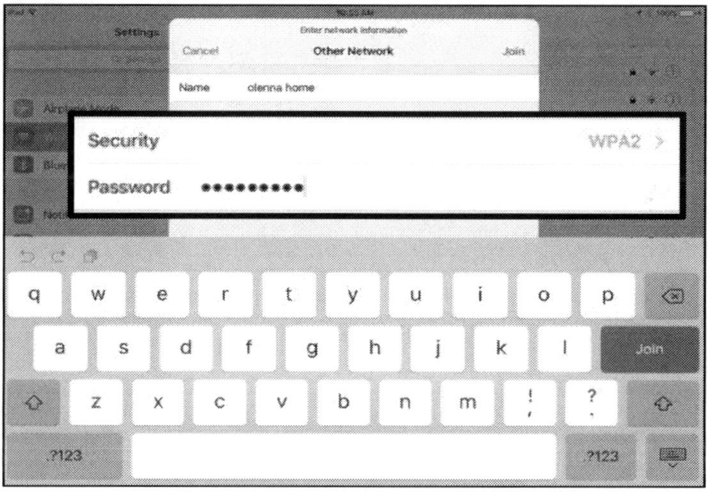

If the network does not appear in the list, it may be out of range or the network may be closed (ie hidden). To connect to a private network, tap More and follow the steps to connect. You need to know the name of the network, security settings and passwords.

Apple ID

If you've already turned on your iPad, you know that Apple ID is part of the installation process. But what else does it do?

In other words, your Apple ID is a simple username and password. It's free to create, but it's an important part of the iPad experience. It's not just an ID on your device, it's also a gateway to other Apple services like the App Store, iCloud, and some built-in apps. The more you use the iPad, the more you can see how popular Apple IDs are.

If you do not have an Apple ID yet, there are plenty of opportunities to create one when setting up your device. You can also register online.

CHAPTER 6: SIRI

Siri is a handy feature that comes with your iPhone. It's also accessible on iPad and the apple desktop computer, Mac Studio. You can check out how to use Siri on Mac studio from chapter 7 of our book 'Mac Studio User Guide by Henry K Mills'.

Steps in installing Siri on iPhone and iPad

- On the Home screen, press Setting .
- Click '**Siri & Search**'
- Tap '**Listen to Hey Siri**' Switch to turn it on.

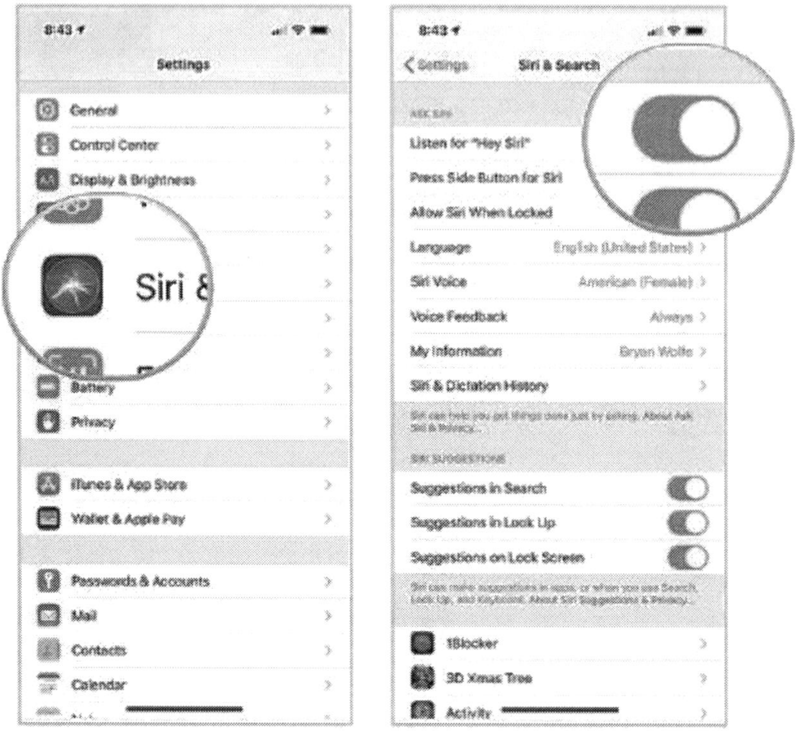

Training "Hey Siri" to know your voice

Whether it's part of the installation process or beyond, it needs to be trained to recognize your voice as soon as you turn on Hey Siri.

- Tap Continue on the Hey Siri settings page where you were.
- Use your voice to say "Hey Siri".
- Use your voice to say, "Hey Siri, help me send a message."

- Use your voice to say, "Hi Siri, how is the weather today?"
- Say "Hey Siri, set the timer to 3 minutes".
- Say, "Hey Siri, play a song."
- On the Hey Siri Ready page, tap Done.

Congratulations! Siri knows your voice now. She is ready to carry out all your commands.

How to use "Hey Siri!"?

With Voice

It's easy to learn how to install Siri, and using "Hey Siri!" that magnificent design, is very easy! You just need to say "Hey Siri" to start the conversation.
Stay within audible range from the iPhone or iPad. Then say "Hey Siri!" just loud enough for your iPhone or iPad to hear your voice.
Tell Siri what you want to do, such as "call my mom through the loudspeaker", "book dinner" or "what is the weather like in Bermuda?"
If you'll like to ask a different question or Maybe have Siri do something else for you, just tap the Siri button or say "Hey Siri".

With Button

First switch on **Press Top Button for Siri:** Do this

- On the Home screen, press Setting.
- Click '**Siri & Search**'

- Tap '**Press Top Button for Siri**' Switch to turn it on.

Next summon Siri with the top button: Press the top button and keep on holding it till Siri comes up. Then tell Siri what you want to do, such as "call my mom through the loudspeaker", "book dinner" or "what is the weather like in Bermuda?"

CHAPTER 7: EXCITING NEW FEATURES IN IPAD OS 16

Apple keeps upgrading the iPadOS. With the new iPadOS 16, there are several exciting new features to look forward to. If you're long time iPad user, prepare to receive these fresh and invigorating iPadOS 16 features. If you're new, don't worry, we'll teach you how to use them within this book.

Home screen Widgets: You can now place a gadget next to your iPad home screen apps. Choose the right gadget sizes, including the new larger size for the iPad

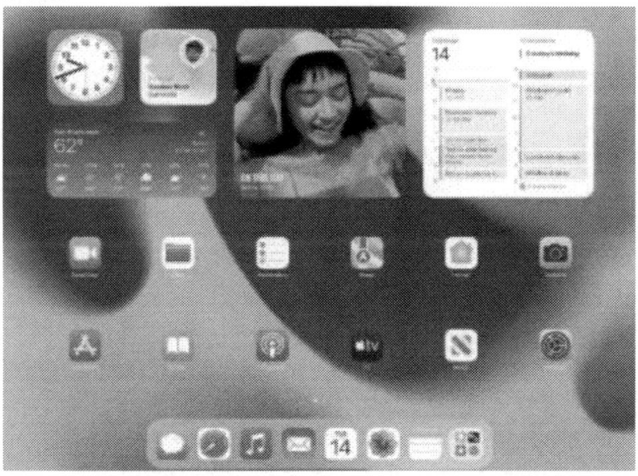

Fig 38. Home Screen Widgets

Application Library: *T*he Application Library automatically organizes your applications into useful categories, such as productivity and games.

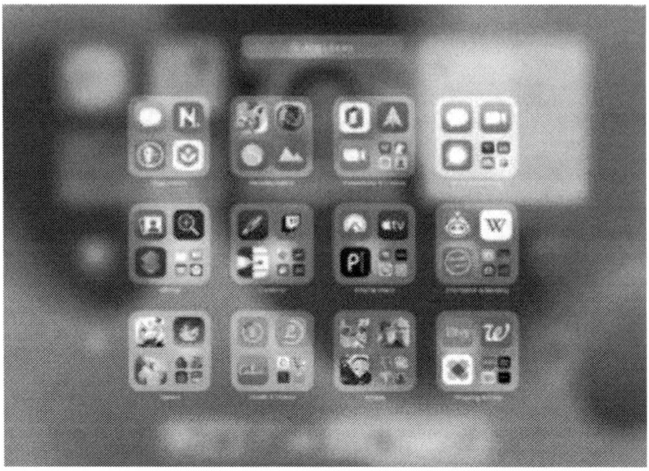

Fig 39. Application Library

Facetime voice isolation mode: Use FaceTime audio splitting to minimize background noise and portrait mode to focus on your graphics. The *grid view* shows the people in your group

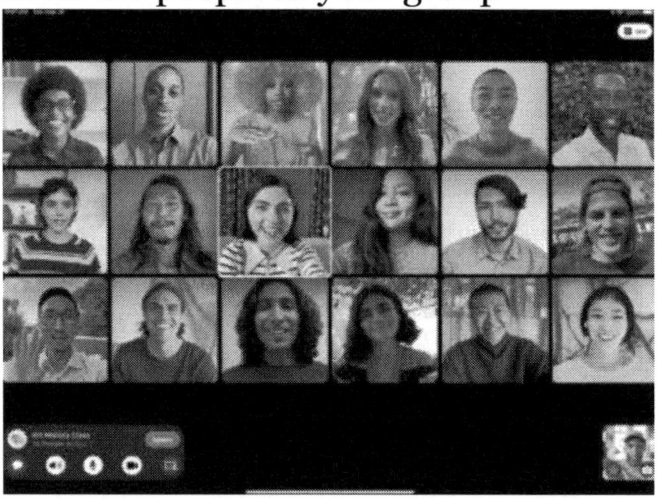

Fig 40. A FaceTime Group call

SharePlay: You can use SharePlay with FaceTime to connect with friends and family. You can watch

TV shows and movies together, listen to music together, and share your screen.

Focus: Focus is used to automatically filter alerts based on what you do. Select a focus candidate such as Work, Sleep, or Personal, and then select the notification you want to receive at that time. When someone outside the scope of the allowed alert tries to contact you, they will see your focus on the message so they know you are busy.

Notifications: Your notifications have been given a new look, contact photos, and a large application icon for easier recognition.

Messages: You can find message links, photos, and other content that you share through messaging in the new Sharing section of the app (available in Photos, Safari, Podcasts, Apple Music, Apple News, or Apple TV).

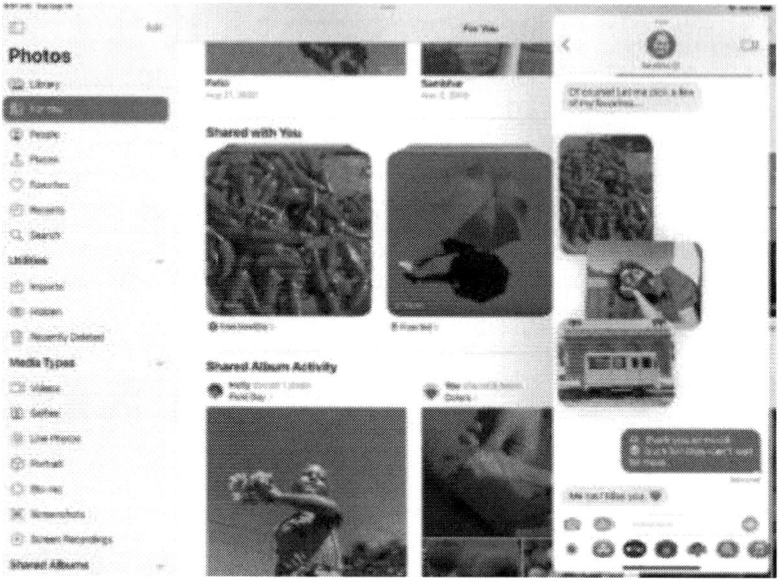

Fig 41. Inserting pictures to Messages

Memoji: Reflects your look and style in new ways. Choose from new costumes for Memoji stickers, more hats and updated tailoring options.

Map: The new interactive globe displays detailed information about mountains, deserts, forests, oceans and more. Detailed maps of cities such as San Francisco and New York show altitude, landmarks, trees, corners, sidewalks and more. The new guide map shows details such as traffic conditions and incidents, and the Route Planner lets you see your upcoming trips.

Visual *Look Up*: Visual Search identifies objects in images, such as popular landmarks, plants, books, and artwork, and provides additional images and information about objects from the Web (US only).

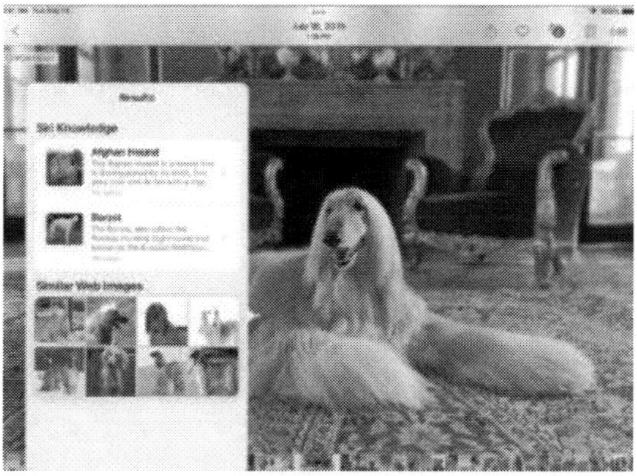

Fig 42. Using Visual Look Up to check a Dog's species

The image is full screen. Inside the image is a dog and above the dog there is a visual search icon showing a section of Siri Knowledge with detailed information about the dog breed, as well as similar web images showing different images of the dog breed.

Quick Notes: Record any application or screenshots that are open on your iPad. You can quickly start your notes by swiping your finger or the Apple Pencil from the bottom right corner of the screen or by opening the Control Center. Quick notes are stored in the Notes application and can contain text, handwriting, links and tags

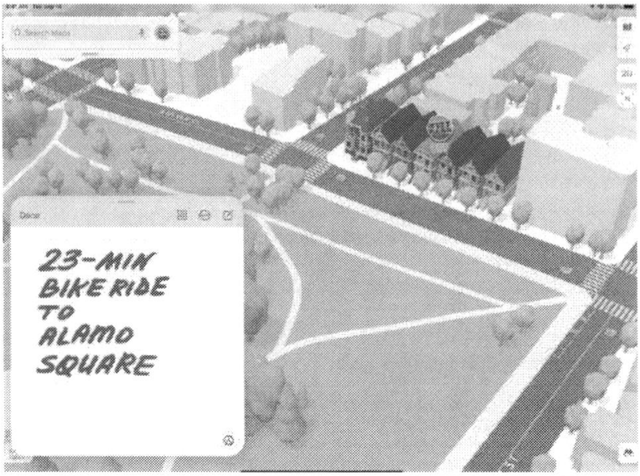

Universal Control: Using a keyboard, mouse, or touchpad, work seamlessly between your Mac and iPad.

ICloud+*:* iCloud+ combines all the features of iCloud with new features, such as iCloud Private Relay (Beta), a service that protects your internet privacy. Hide My Email is an easy way to create an arbitrary email address when filling out a web form. We also have enhanced support for secure HomeKit video recording so you can install more security cameras at home.

Hide My Mail: You can use this feature to keep your personal email address private by signing up for iCloud+. Hide My Email creates a unique, random email address that will be forwarded to your personal email account.

Screen time messages*: C*an detect nude photos before they are sent or received on your child's device and provide useful resources.

Security: The Digital Legacy app lets you define certain individuals as Legacy contacts who can open your iCloud accounts and personal information in case you die.
Accessibility*:* Customize the display settings and text size of each application. You can zoom in on the text, use bold, increase the contrast, and rotate the colors to fit exactly the application you need. Use VoiceOver to take a closer look at people, objects, text and graphics in your photos. *It also* covers unwanted environmental or external noise by playing a continuous, pleasant background sound. Hide surround sound by navigating to adjust accessibility settings for a specific application, explore photos, and play background sounds on your iPad.
Learn the secrets of iPadOS: The new **Tips application** often add new suggestions to help you get the most out of your iPad.

CHAPTER 8: USING THE KEYBOARD

The iPad has a built-in virtual keyboard that you can use to enter text on your device. Like we said in the introductory chapters, you can get a physical keyboard to attach to your iPad. But that may not be necessary, since the iPad's virtual keyboard has everything you'll need, plus shortcuts to ease typing

To Open the Keyboard:

Each time you tap a text box, you see the iPad virtual keyboard. For example, you will see the keyboard when writing an email, writing a comment, or entering a web address.

Getting to Know the Keyboard

The keyboard has several keys and features you will love to know about. Some of these include:

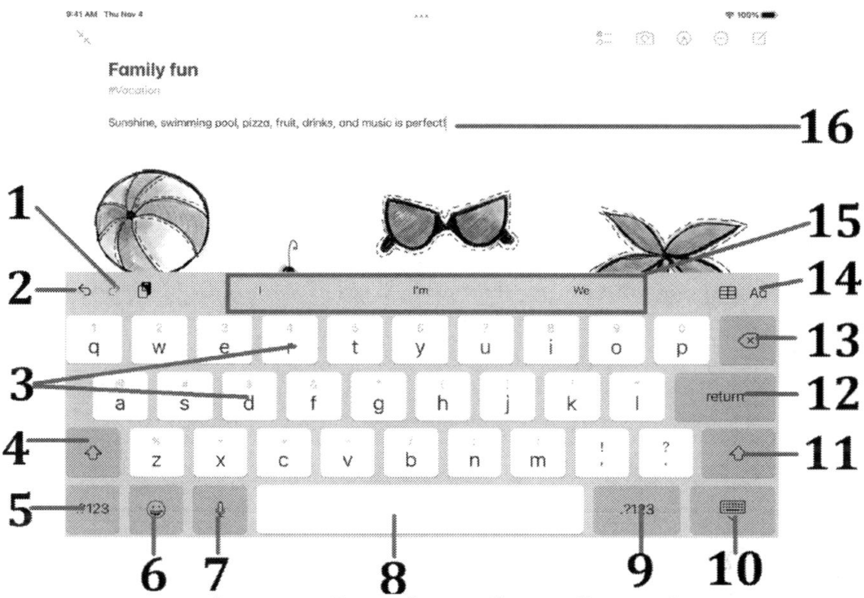

Fig 43. The Virtual Keyboard

1. *Redo*
2. *Undo*
3. *Letter keys*
4. *Shift*
5. *Numbers*
6. *Emoji*
7. *Dictation*
8. *Space*
9. *Numbers*
10. *Hide keyboard*
11. *Shift*
12. *Return*
13. *Backspace*
14. *Font*
15. *Predictive Text*
16. *Cursor*

- **Cursor**: Cursor indicates where the text appears.
- **Backspace key:** Tap the Backspace key to delete the letters to the left of the cursor. To delete the entire word, press and hold the Backspace key.
- **Predictive text:** iPad will create automated text based on what you're writing and what you've written in the past. Click on a word to enter it.
- **Letter key:** The body of the keyboard contains the letter keys and the space bar. Tap this key to add the desired text.
- **Shift key:** Tap the Shift key, then tap a letter to enter a capital letter or another letter. Double-click the Shift key to turn on Caps Lock.
- **Hide keyboard:** Click here to hide the keyboard. You can display the keyboard again by clicking on any text box.
- **Space bar:** Tap the space bar to add a space. Double clicking the space at the end of a sentence also adds a full stop automatically.
- **Voice Dictation:** With this feature, you can create a text just by speaking, without typing on the keyboard. Tap the microphone icon on your keyboard to start talking.
- **Emoji keyboard:** Tap here to switch your keyboard from text to emoji.
- **Numbers and special characters:** Tap here to switch the keyboard from letters to

numbers or special characters. Press the button again to go back. You can also add a space after the character to recover it.

- **Undo**: Click here to revert the last change you made
- **Redo**: Click here to go back to a previous change you've undone.
- **Return**: Click here to enter a new paragraph.
- **Fonts**: Click here to change your font options like bold, italics, & size.

Keyboard functions

The iPad Virtual Keyboard includes several features that make typing into your device faster and easier.

Suggestion

iPad suggests special words as you type. When writing, you can use suggestions simply by tapping the space bar. In the example below, we used the proposal to change 'agreem' to agreement. To reject a proposal, ignore the proposal and continue writing.

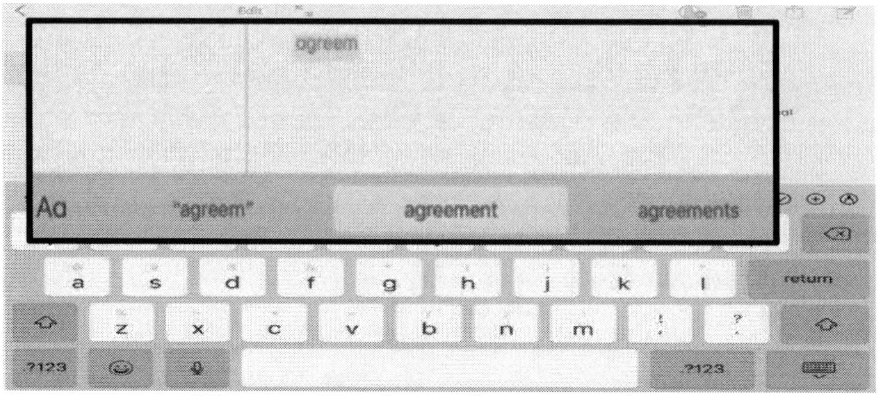

Fig 44. Keyboard suggestions

Automatic correction

iPad will automatically correct common spelling errors. For example, **teh** will be converted to **the**. This is a powerful feature, but auto-correction is not perfect. It's also automatic so you don't always notice when something changes. You should always check the text to make sure it is correct.

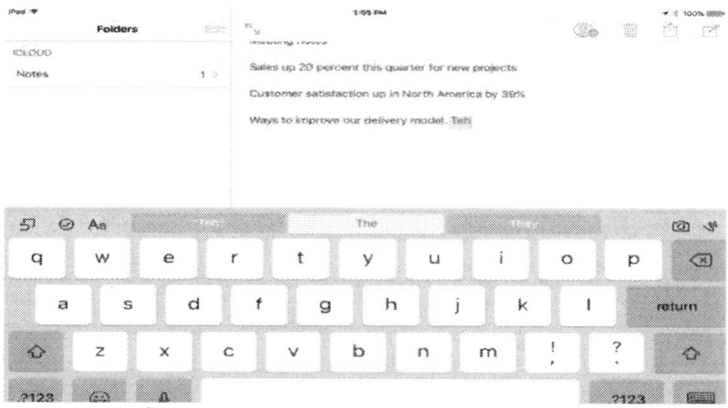

Fig 45. Automatic Correction

Error Search

In addition to automatic correction, iPad detects spelling errors as you type. Your iPad will underline any word having a spelling error with red color. Tap words to see suggestions for possible spelling mistakes. A list of possible spellings is displayed. You can replace the existing word by simply clicking on the suggestion.

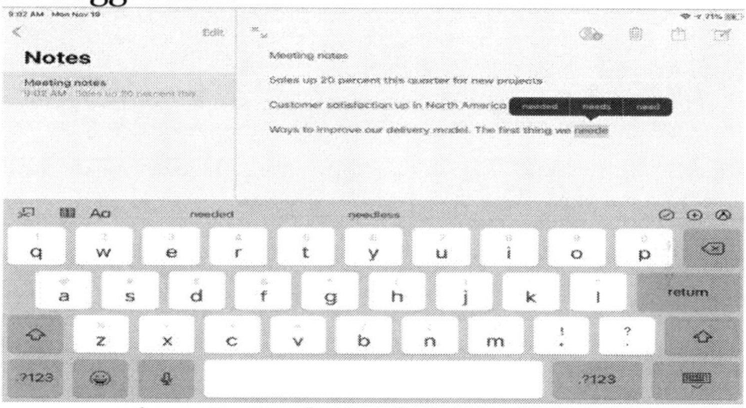

Fig 46. Keyboard Error Search

Move the cursor

Sometimes you want to change something at the beginning of a sentence or paragraph. Instead of deleting existing text and starting over, you can move the cursor to the desired location. To move the cursor, just tap on the desired location.

If you need more control, hold down the screen and then drag the magnifying glass (without releasing your finger), to select the cursor.

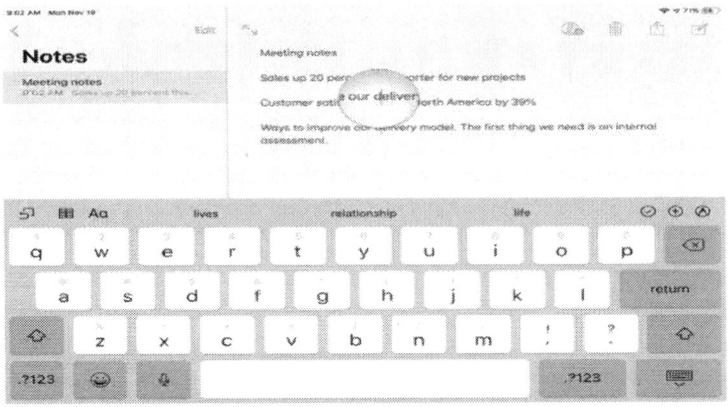

Fig 47. Moving the Cursor

To copy and paste the text

If you want to move the text from one place to another, you can copy and paste it. This is especially useful when transferring text between different applications. For example, you can find useful information in Safari, copy it and paste it into your Notes app.

First you need to select the text you want to copy. Double-click the screen next to the text you want to select and drag the selection handle to select the text.

Menu options such as cut, copy and paste appear above the selected text. Tap Copy.

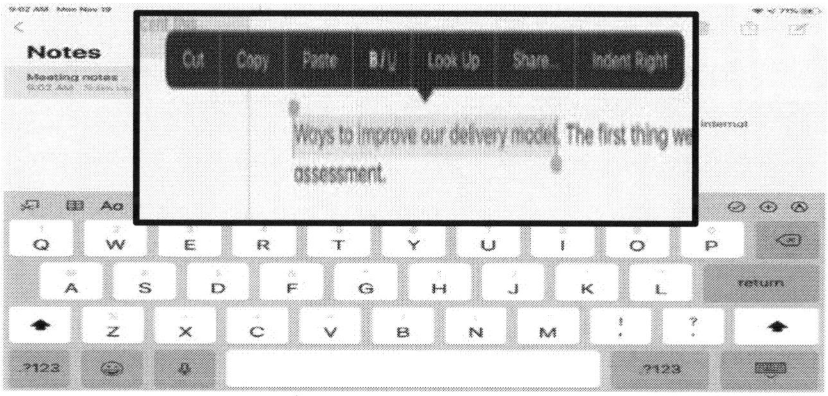

Fig 48. Copy Text

Double-tap the desired place in the text, then tap Paste.

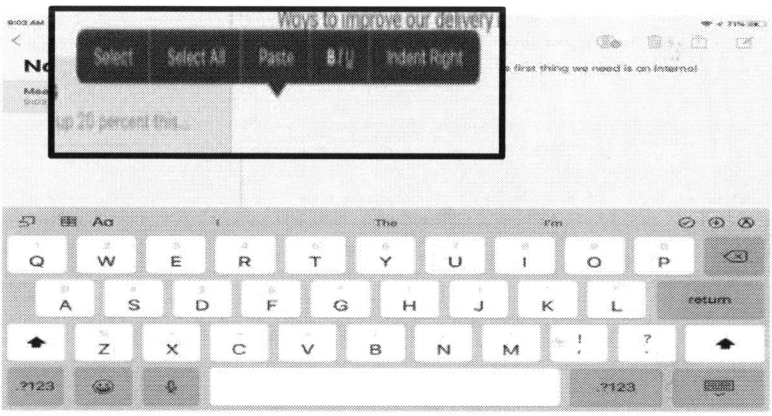

Fig 49. Paste Text

The copied text is displayed.

Other keyboard Tricks

The keyboard has many other features that are not immediately apparent. Below are some of the most important ones.

Orientation of the Keyboard: You can rotate the iPad to resize the keyboard. The keyboard uses about half of the screen in landscape mode and about a quarter of the screen in portrait mode.

Other characters: You can add accents or other characters by holding down a specific letter or symbol.

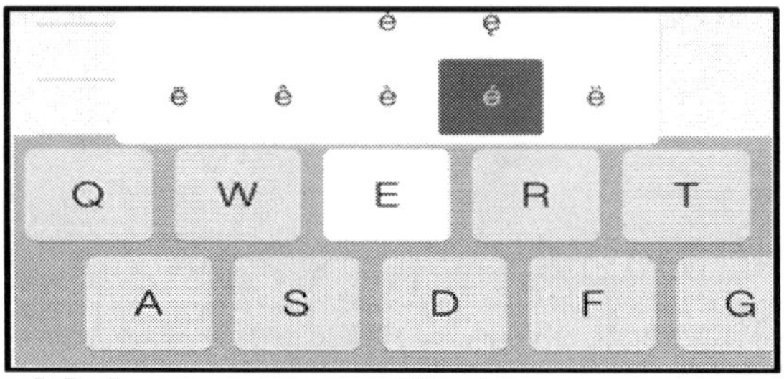

Fig 50. Hold down a specific letter or symbol. Click a special character.

Undo button: Instead of deleting the text manually, you can use the Undo button. Simply tap the number key and select Cancel.

Swipe to enter: If you only need to enter one number or special character, press and hold the number key, and press and hold on the screen to select the character you want.

CHAPTER 9: BROWSE THE INTERNET WITH SAFARI

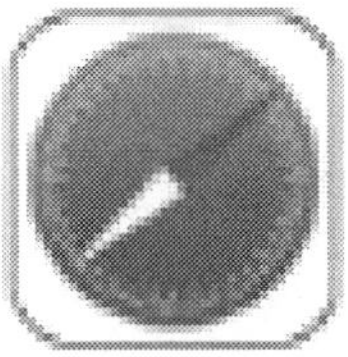

What is Safari?

Safari is a browser built into the iPad. It's similar to other browsers like Google Chrome or Internet Explorer. Use this to access the webpage on your device. Safari's interface is similar to that found in desktop browsers, and it also has some unique features that make mobile browsers easier.

To open Safari, press 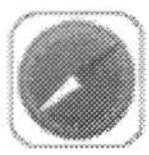 on the home screen.

Get to know Safari

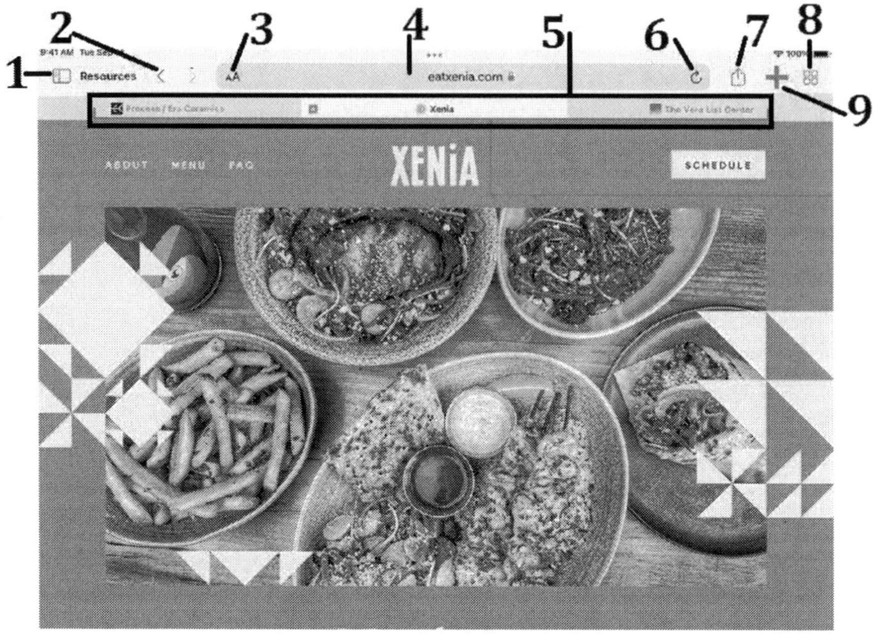

Fig 51. Safari interface

1. *Bookmarks, reading lists, Shared links*
2. *Navigation buttons*
3. *Font Options*
4. *Address Bar*
5. *Open Tabs*
6. *Refresh*
7. *Share*
8. *Show all Tabs*
9. *Add New Tab*

- **Navigation buttons:**

Use the back and forth buttons to scroll between recently visited pages.

- **Bookmark or reading list or shared link:**

Tap here to view bookmarks, shared web pages and reading lists. You can read web pages that you have added to your reading list even if you are not connected to the internet.

- **Reader:**

The Reader feature allows you to view your web articles in large, easy-to-read format without any ads or clutter.

- **Address bar:**

The address bar appears with the URL of the current page. To go to a new page, just enter the new address. This bar can also be utilized for browsing

- **Refresh**: Tap here to refresh. Or swipe your screen down from the top.
- **Tabs:**

Safari simplifies multitasking by allowing you to browse and open links on separate tabs. To go to another tab, tap the tab you want. Tap X to close the tab.

- **Share button:**

You can use the Share button to create bookmarks and save pages to your reading list. You can also email the link to your friends or share it on Twitter and Facebook.

- **New tab button:**

Tap here to create a new tab. When you create a new tab, Favorites will appear. This site contains shortcuts to the web pages you visit most often. You can click on the web page to go to that page or enter the URL in the address bar.

- **Show all tabs button:**

Click the Show All Tabs button to see thumbnails of all open tabs.

Browsing Online

Safari includes several features that make browsing the web easier. We have put together some of the most useful features below.

Open links in new tabs

Once you have found a link to a website of your choice, you can open it in a new tab. This allows you to browse the linked site without losing the location of the original page.
To open a link in a new tab, press and hold, and select Open in new tab.

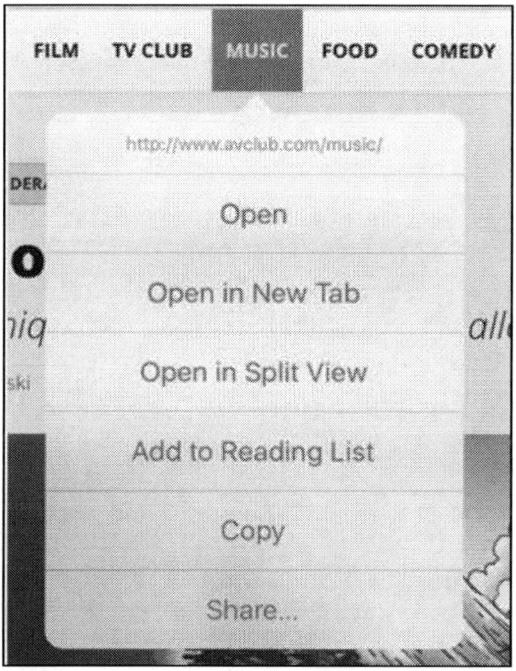

Fig 52. Open links in new tabs

Multi-touch zoom

It can be difficult to read web pages in Safari. Fortunately, there are two ways to zoom in and out using multi-touch gestures.

- **Double-tap the screen**: This gesture expands to the area of the screen that is clicked. This is especially useful when reading small text. Double-click again to zoom out.
- **Screen Pinch**: This gesture allows you to zoom in and out to gain more control over the screen size of your page.

Screen direction

Remember that you can turn your iPad at any time to change the orientation of the screen. While some sites appear better in portrait view, others are better in landscape.

Add a web page to your home screen

If you visit the same website frequently, we recommend that you bookmark it. If you want faster access, you can add icons to the home screen home page. Simply tap the Share button, select Add Home screen and click Add.

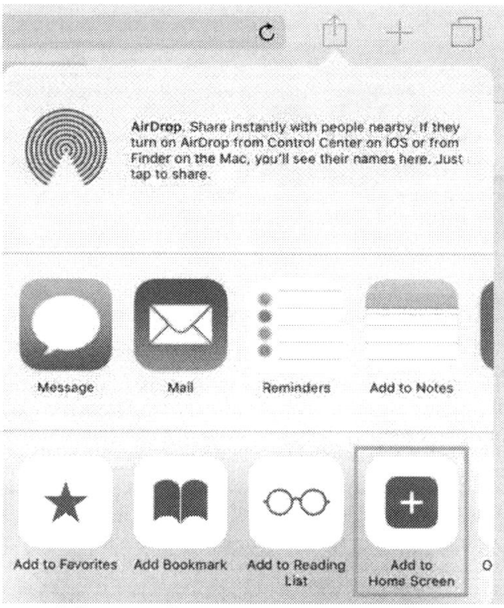

Fig 53. Add a web page to your home screen

This page appears as an icon in the home screen. Tap the icon to open Safari and display the webpage.

Use Split View to view two pages

You can use the All Tabs button to open two blank pages or links in split view at once.
If you want to open blank pages with Split View, touch the All Tabs button and hold it till a menu shows. Click **New Window on Split View**.
If you want to open links with Split View, touch your link and hold it till a menu shows. Then click **Open on Split View.**

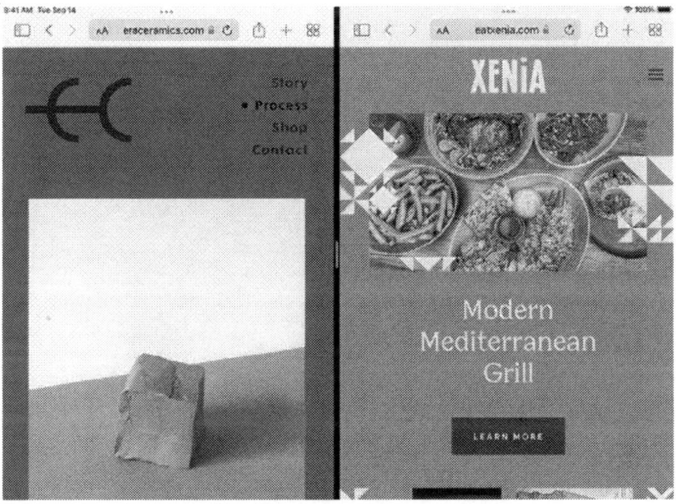

Fig 54. Split View

To carry one of the windows to the opposite site of your Split View, Touch the three dots by the Up of that window. Push it to either left or right.
If you instead want to go back to viewing only one tab, push the black line separating the tabs to the side of the window you'll like to close.

When you now want to close both Split View tabs, touch the All Tabs button ⊞ button again and hold till the split view closes.

CHAPTER 10: SETTINGS

Security and general settings

Once you get used to the iPad, please take some time to review and customize your device settings. Settings control everything from how the iPad works to the data it shares with apps and other devices. You can access the settings by tapping the icon 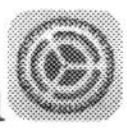 on the home screen.

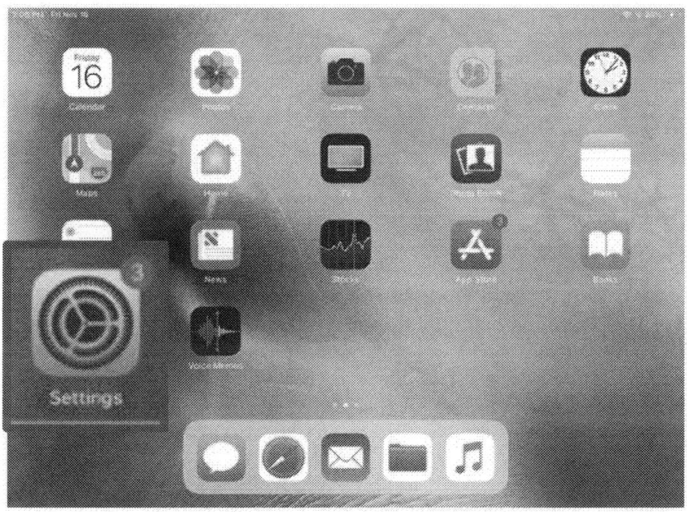

Fig 55. Tap Settings

Settings allow you to easily access various items, such as notifications and privacy settings. This chapter will cover Touch ID and password, General, and privacy settings.

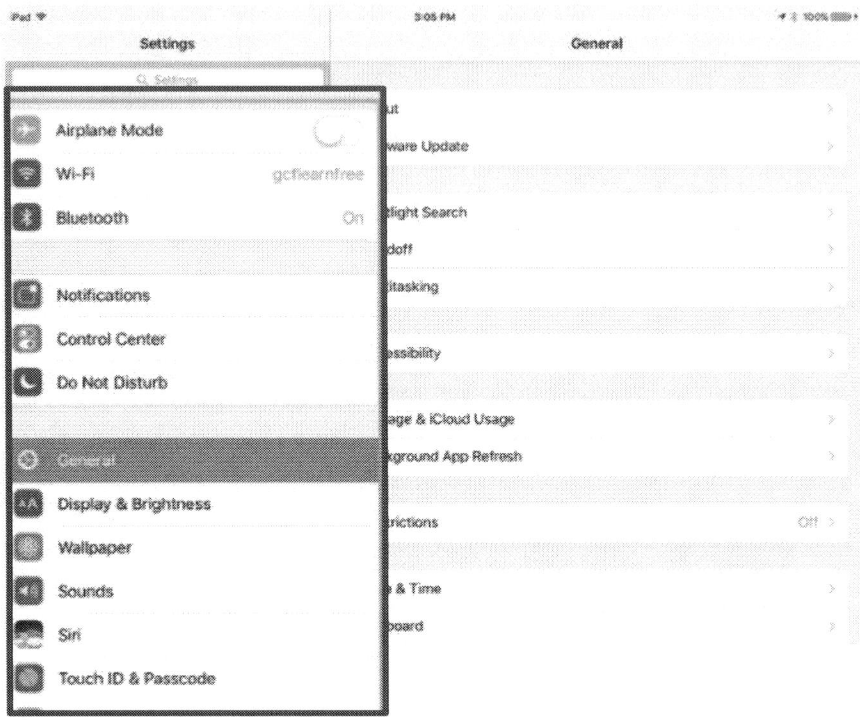

Touch ID and password

With Touch ID and password, you can customize the security to unlock your iPad. Normally, a passcode is needed if you want to unlock your iPad. You can also unlock your iPad using a fingerprint with a feature called Touch ID.

To change the password lock:

The first time you start your iPad, you will be prompted to create a passcode lock. If you want to change it, you can easily change it with these simple steps.

- From Home screen, press Settings
- Scroll through, and then tap **Touch ID and password**.
- Tap **Change password**.
- Use the keypad to enter the current passcode.
- The following screen will automatically appear asking you to enter your new password. Enter your new password. (You are going to have to fill it in twice to confirm.)

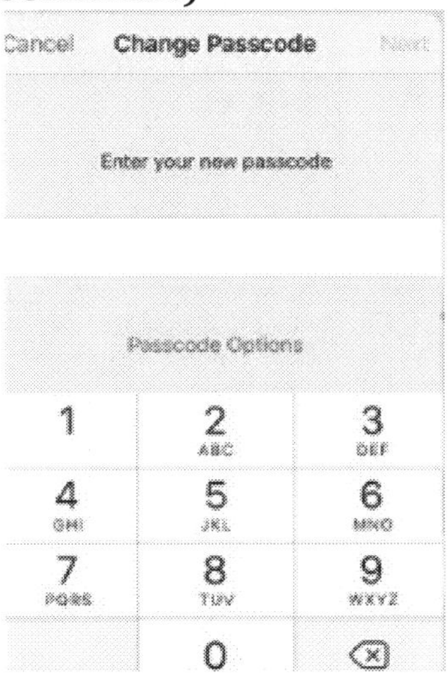

Fig 56. Enter your new password.

- A new password will be set.

To Activate Touch ID

You can also set your iPad to open with your fingerprint. Instead of entering your password, just put your finger on the Top button.

- From the iPad's home screen, press Setting

- Scroll through, and then tap **Touch ID and password**.
- Type in your **password** and click on **Add fingerprint**

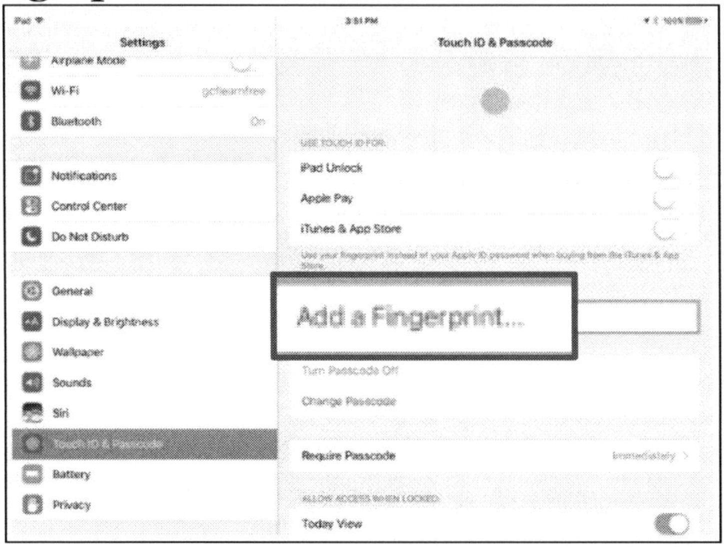

Fig 57. Click on Add fingerprint

- Follow the instructions on the screen and place your finger or thumb on the TOP button. Until the iPad reads your fingerprint well you need to touch the TOP button repeatedly.
- Fingerprint will be added and you will be able to unlock your phone with Touch ID.

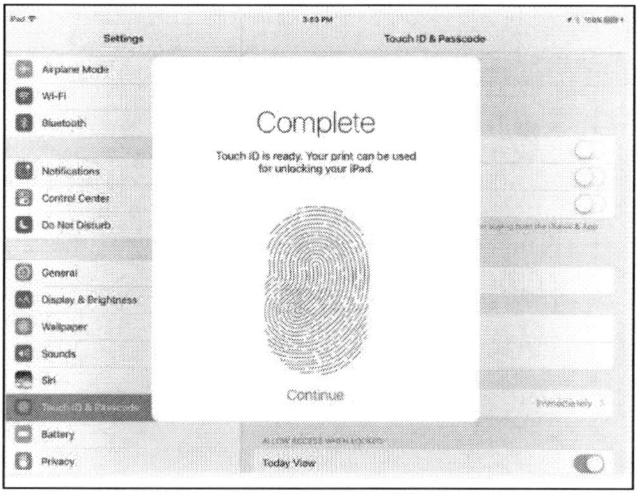

Fig 58. Touch ID set

- You can add multiple fingerprints to Touch ID and use any number of fingers or thumbs to unlock your iPad.

General

In general, it allows you to customize settings that control storage, accessibility, and overall settings.

Use screen time to set limits

Restrictions act as parental controls. You can use this feature to limit the amount of time your kids spend on their iPad. You can also set a passcode to ensure they don't change your settings. You can even block access to adult websites and inappropriate content. You can turn restrictions on or change them in the Screen time section of the settings menu.

- From the iPad's home screen, press Setting 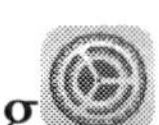

- Scroll through, and then tap **Screen Time**.
- Then tap '**Turn on Screen Time**'.
- Tap 'This is my child's iPad'.

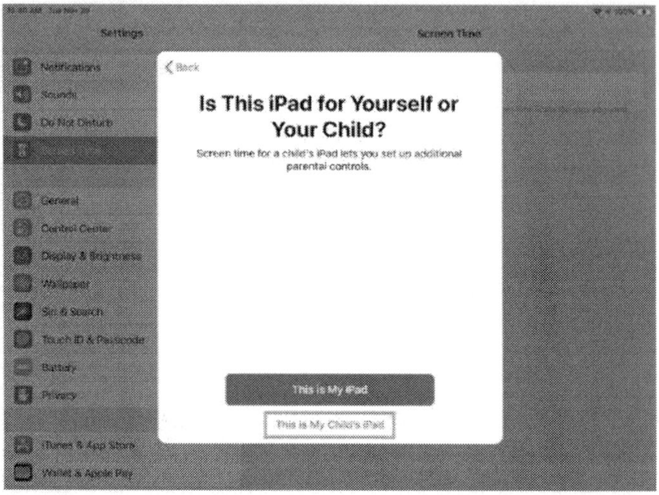

Fig 59. Tap 'This is my child's iPad'

- **Downtime**: Set the Start and End times when your child can use the iPad, then tap 'Set Down time'.

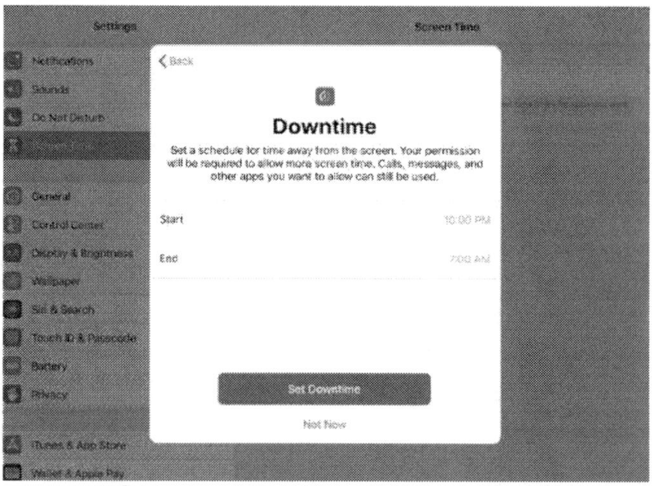

Fig 60. Tap 'Set Down time'

- **App Limits**: Select the category you want to set a time limit for your child, then tap **Set application limit**.

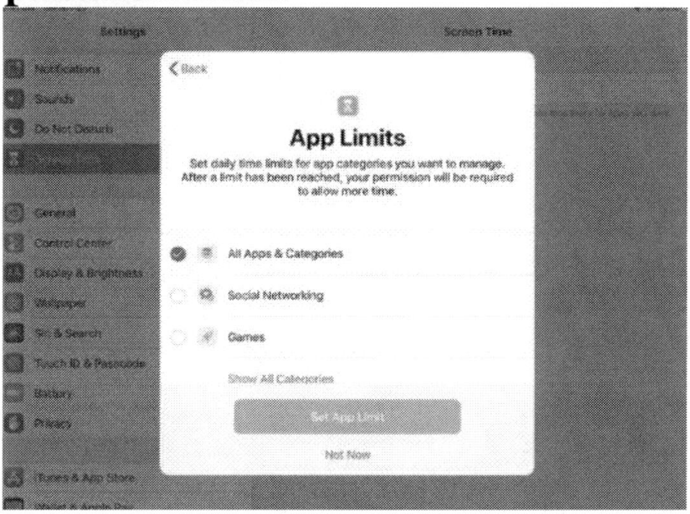

Fig 61. Tap Set Apps Limits

- Enter a passcode that you can use to unlock iPad if you want to change the display time settings or allow your child to spend more time on their device.

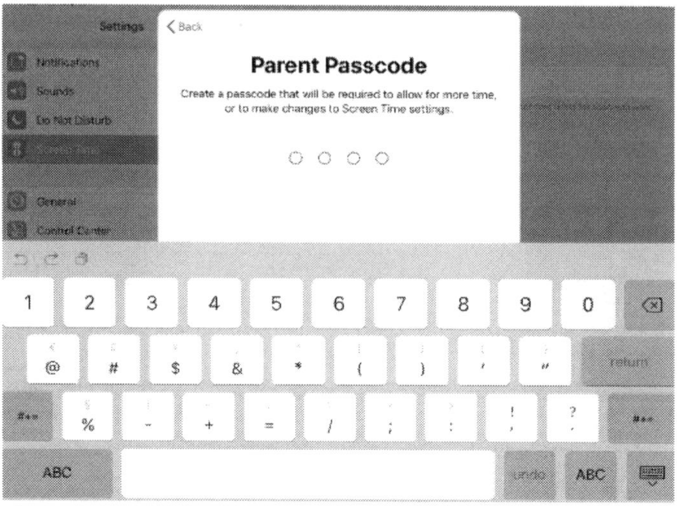

- You're done.

At any time, you can access and change advanced settings in the Screen time section of the Settings menu.

- From your iPad's home screen, press Setting 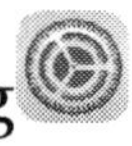
- Scroll through, and then tap **Screen Time**.
- You'll find four Categories:
  - Downtime: Set when you want your child to Stop using his/her device (e.g. at bedtime, at school, etc.)
  - App Limits: From here you can adjust how long your child spends on selected Apps.
  - Always Allowed: Select essential Apps you want your child to always have access to, even during Downtime (for example, Phone app, Messages, etc. just in case of an emergency).
  - Contents & Privacy Restrictions: From here you can choose to block offensive websites that

feature things like pornography, violence, racist ideas and others.

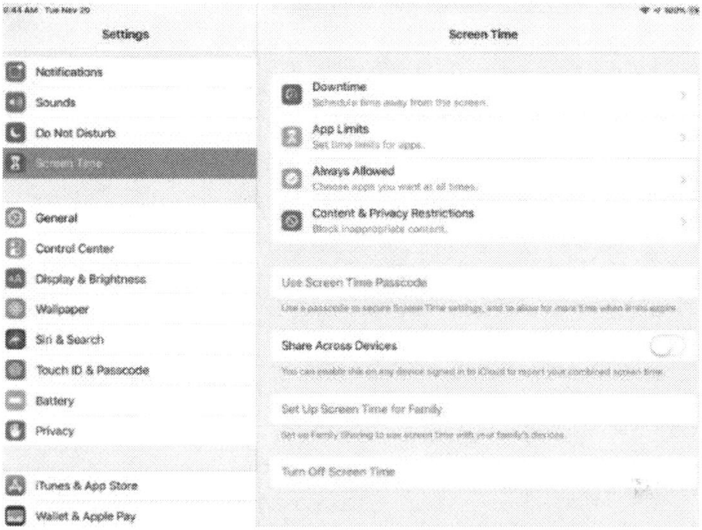

Fig 62. Screen Time Options

- If you're using the same Apple ID on both your tab and other Apple devices (iPhones, Macs, iPods, etc.), you can switch on (green) **Share Across Devices**, to apply your new settings across board.

Software update

Software Update is the place to download iOS updates from Apple. Updates often include bug fixes and other enhancements designed to improve the iPad experience. If there is an update, click on 'Software Update', then click the Install key.

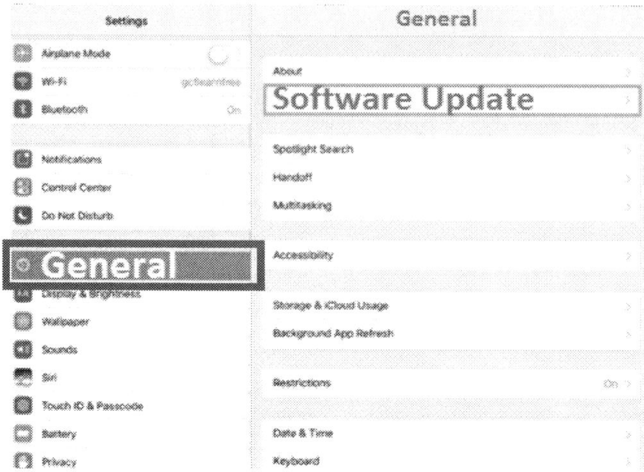

Fig 63- Software Update

Privacy

Third-party applications may request access to your personal information. For example, your app might ask for access to your Twitter account to make it easier for you to share things with your friends. Another application may request access to your contacts to help you connect with your acquaintances.

The application will ask for permission before opening your information for the first time. However, these settings can be managed in privacy at any time.

To manage your privacy settings:

- From your iPad's home screen, press on the Settings key 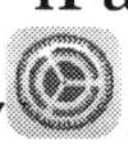.

- Tap **Privacy** in the left pane.
- Tap the item to see the application (if any) that requested access to the information.

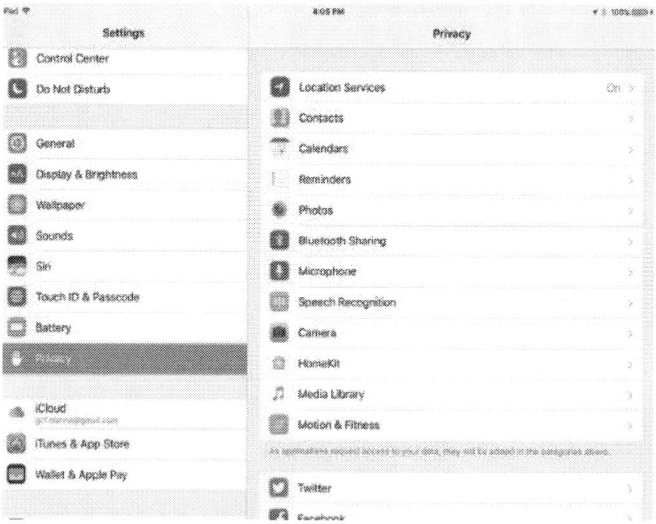

Fig 64- Privacy

- Turn controls on or off to allow or disable access to selected apps.

To restrict ad tracking:

Some third-party applications may use information from your iPad to serve **targeted ads** based on your interests. These are based on how you use your iPad, such as your browsing history and installed applications. If you do not want targeted ads, you can restrict the tracking of your ads. This feature does not limit the number of ads you receive. It only stops the use of your personal information by third parties.

- From your iPad's home screen, press on the Settings key .
- Tap **Privacy** in the left pane.
- Once you've opened Privacy, tap Advertising.
- Click on and enable the checkbox to restrict ad tracking.

WALLPAPER AND RINGTONES

As you learned on security and general settings, there are many ways to customize your iPad. If you want to make your iPad more personal, we recommend that you choose your own wallpaper or change the sound effects.

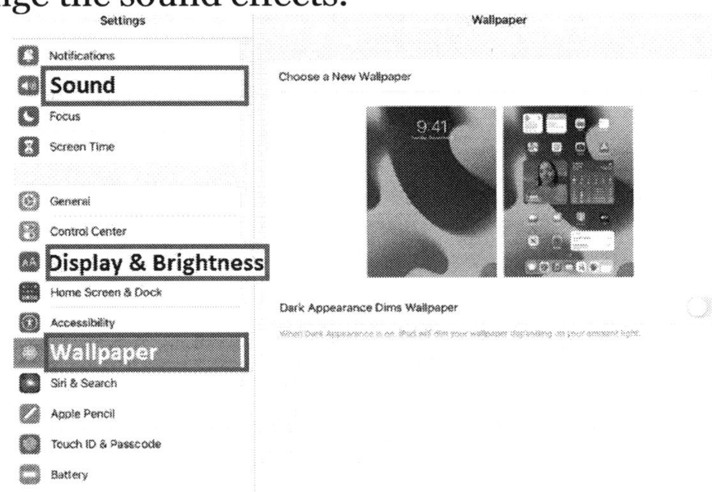

Fig 65. Sound, Brightness, Wallpaper

Remember that you can access the settings by tapping the icon on the home screen. In this section, we are going to focus the following settings:

- Wallpaper: From here you can customize your iPad wallpaper to fit your background and lock screen.
- Screen and brightness: From here you can customize the display settings and brightness of your iPad.
- Sound: From here you can customize the sound of your iPad.

Wallpaper

Change the wallpaper!
You can add your own wallpaper to personalize your iPad.

- From your iPad's home screen, press Setting .
- Tap **Wallpaper** in the left pane.
- Tap '**Choose a New Wallpaper**'.
- Tap **Dynamic** or **Stills** to check out the built-in wallpaper that came with your iPad, or select a photo on your device from the albums below. In this example, tap Stills.

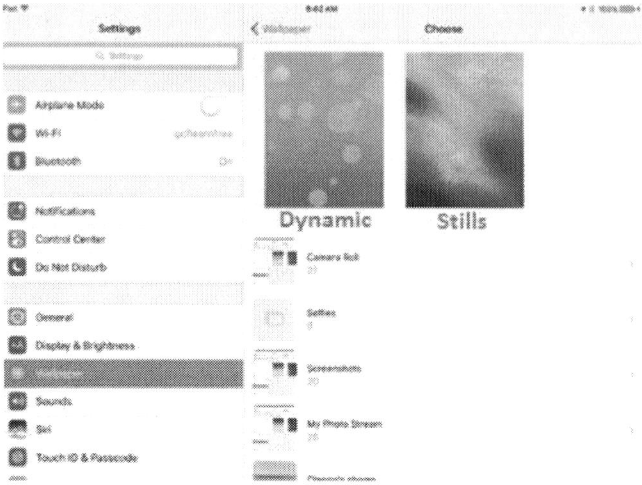

Fig 66. Tap Dynamic or Stills

- Tap the image to open the full screen preview.

Use the menu bar to place wallpaper on your **Lock screen**, **Home screen**, or **both**. Tap Cancel to cancel the preview without changing the wallpaper.

Set wallpaper from the Photo application

If you are already viewing photos in the Photos app, you can set any photo as wallpaper without opening Settings. Simply select your photo, tap the Share button in the bottom left corner and select **Use as wallpaper**.

Screen and brightness

If it is difficult to see the iPad's screen, it is recommended to adjust the brightness of the screen. Decreasing the screen brightness can also help extend battery life.

- From your iPad's home screen, press Setting .
- Tap **Display & Brightness** in the left pane.
- Drag the slider from the Display and Brightness settings to increase or decrease the screen brightness.

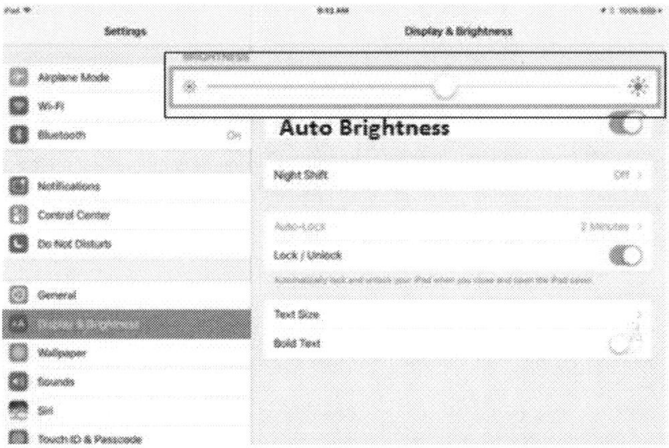

Fig 67. Drag the slider for Brightness

- Auto-Brightness uses a built-in light sensor to automatically adjust the brightness according to the current lighting conditions. You can turn this feature on or off by simply tapping the switch for **Auto Brightness**.
- You can change the brightness at any time from your Control Center:
    - o Simply swipe down from the top right corner of the home screen to access the control panel.
    - o Drag the slider for Brightness to increase or decrease the screen brightness.

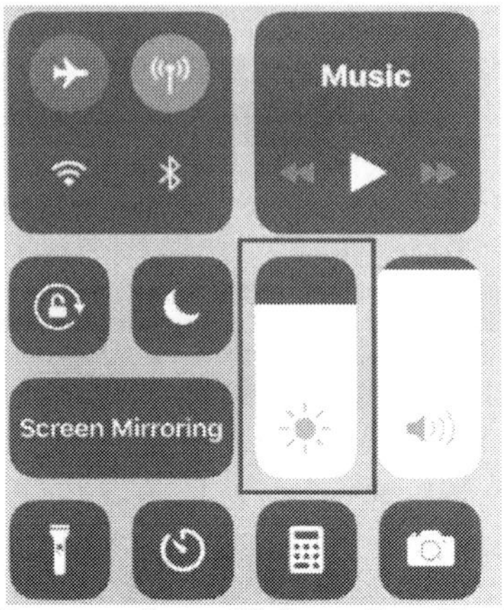

Fig 68. Drag the slider for Brightness

Sound

Sound settings allow you to change sound effects for various alerts (such as new emails and calendar events) and ringtones for the FaceTime app. You can also adjust the volume of these sounds and enable or disable system sound effects such as keyboard clicks and rock sounds.
To change audio settings:

- From your iPad's home screen, press Setting 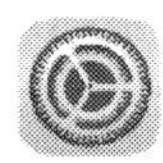 .
- Press **Sound** on the left.
- Customize the sound settings as needed. For example, you can choose a new ringtone for the FaceTime app or a new alert tone for your email. Take the time to try out different sounds and settings to find what you like best.

MANAGING NOTIFICATIONS

Notifications alert you to many things on your iPad, including incoming messages, new emails, calendar events, and more. Notifications behave a little differently depending on the applications, but they are easy to customize. This chapter will show you how to edit the Notification Center and choose which applications will pop up there.

Notification Center

The Notification Center stores all notifications in one place. Just swipe down from the up of the screen to assess it at any time, including from the lock screen.

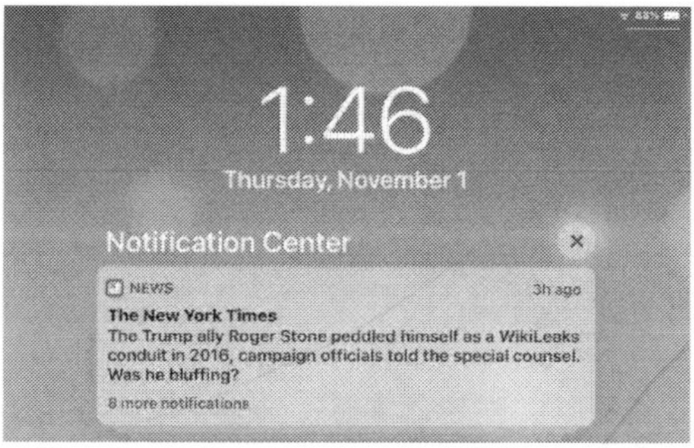

Fig 69. Swipe down to Notification Center

By default, the Notification Center displays recent alerts, starting with the most recent alert. From the Recent Notifications screen, swipe right to access Today's notifications. This includes all calendar events, latest news, weather and more.

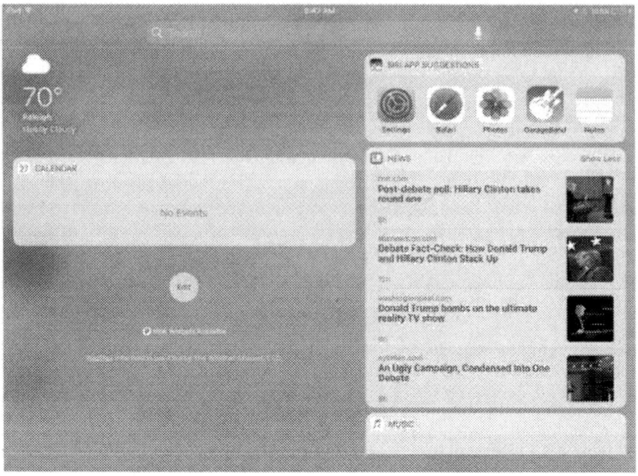

Clear notifications

Notifications will remain in the Notification Center until they are rejected or cleared. To clear the notification, tap X by it, then press Clear.

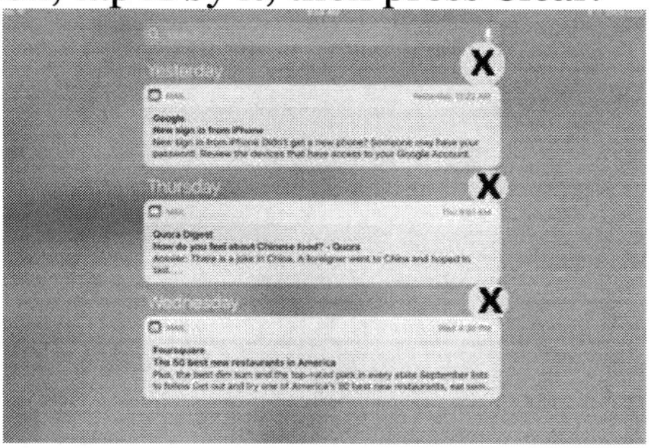

SYNCING YOUR IPAD

Syncing (short for synchronization) makes it easy to keep things updated between your computer, iPad and other mobile devices. This way you can access important files on any device whenever you need them. This chapter describes how to sync iPad using iCloud.

Sync with iCloud

You can sync iPad to iCloud wirelessly. It works in the background and synchronizes important information between various devices. For example, you can buy a song from iTunes on your iPad and listen to it on your Mac computer. Alternatively, you can create a to-do list on your Mac computer and then track it on your iPad.

By syncing your iPad with iCloud, you get access to several features, including:
iCloud Photo Library: This feature synchronizes the latest photos between devices. This means you can take a photo on your iPad and view it instantly on your iPhone or Mac Computer. You can also use this feature to share your photos privately with friends and family.
Find My iPad: If your iPad is lost or stolen, this feature will help you locate your iPad.
Backup and Restore: This feature backs up important files and settings on your iPad, such as apps and messages, to the cloud.
These features are available on iPad and other devices such as iPhone, Mac and iPods.
You are going to need an Apple ID to use iCloud.

To set up iCloud:

- From your iPad's home screen, press Setting .
- Press the name of your account on the top.
- Then tap **iCloud**.

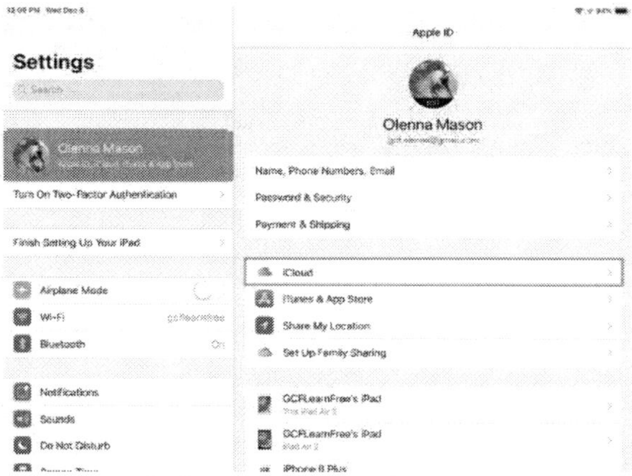

- A list of iCloud features will be displayed. Tap the control to turn each feature on or off as you wish. To get the most out of iCloud, we recommend turning on **ALL** these features.
- To set up automatic backup on iCloud, scroll down and tap **iCloud Backup**. Then switch it to green (On).
- After enabling iCloud Backup, Your iPad will be copied to iCloud whenever it is charging, connected to Wi-Fi and locked.

Installing other devices

If you use iCloud to sync information with other devices (iPhone, iPod Touch, Mac, PC, etc.), you also need to install iCloud on those devices. Visit Apple Support for installation instructions.

If you bought something in the iTunes Store or App Store on another device, you can have it automatically appear on your iPad.
To enable this feature:

- Open **Settings** 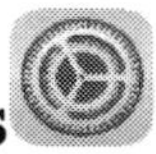
- **Tap iTunes & App Store**
- Then turn on music, apps, books, and audiobooks.

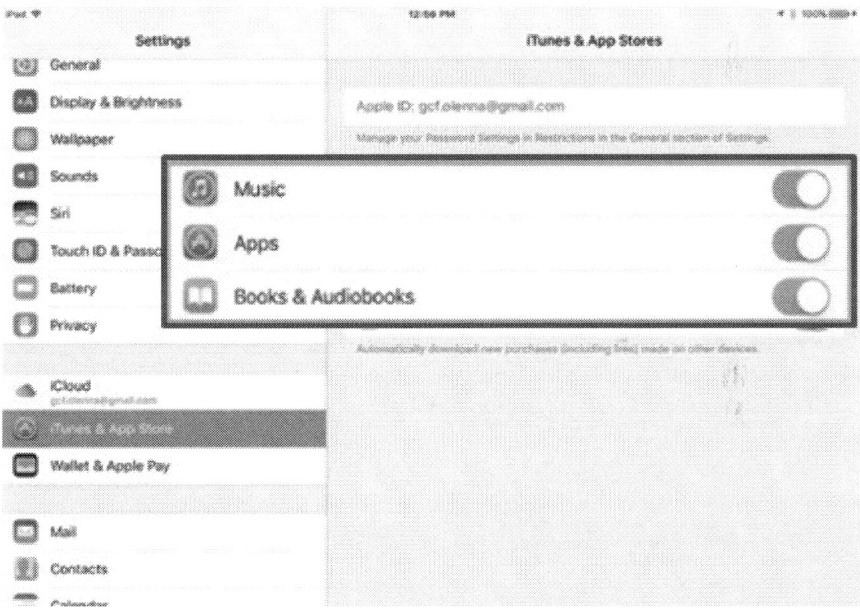

iCloud.com

Even if none of your devices are with you, you can still look up some important iCloud information online. Do this:

- Visit www.icloud.com.
- Fill in your Apple ID.
- Fill in the password to your account.
- Sign in.
- From here, you can view your calendar, search for your devices, and perform other functions.

CHAPTER 11: INSTALLING AND MANAGING APPLICATIONS

Even if you're new to the iPad, you've probably heard of the app (short for application). The idea is simple. An application is a computer program designed to run on your device. The iPad comes with several built-in apps, but you can download more from the App Store. You can also easily manage applications on your device with the iPad.

App Store

In the App Store, you'll find countless applications (apps) you can download for free or buy. From games to entertainment to productivity tools, you'll find everything from apps to help with common tasks like studying for exams, cooking dinners, and monitoring itineraries.

You're going to find countless free apps that can be downloaded for free. Many others cost only $ 0.99, but some are more expensive. If you are not sure which app to try first, you can choose from suggestions in the App Store or view apps that are popular with other iPad users.

What makes up the App Store?

Some features that you'll find in the app store are shown in the diagram below:

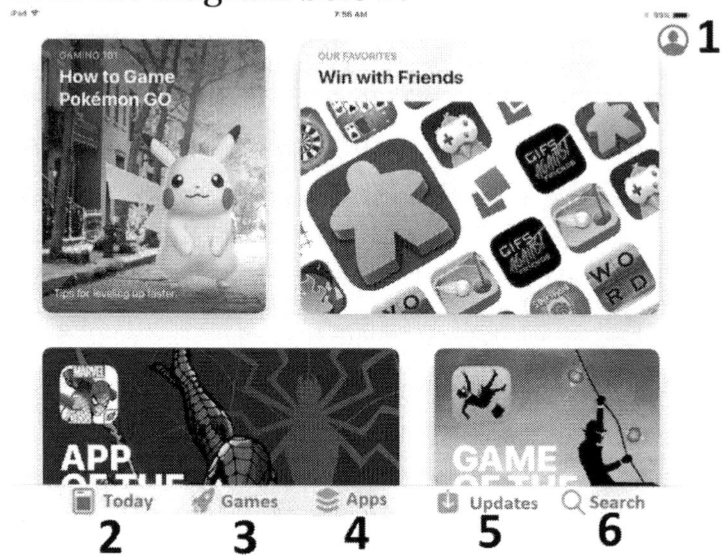

Fig 70. App Store Interface

1. *Account*
2. *Today*
3. *Games*
4. *Apps*
5. *Updates*
6. *Search*

- **Account:**

In the Account menu you can change account options, view purchased apps, used gift cards and more.

- **Today:**

Today the tab is updated daily with the latest apps and games, as well as articles from the App Store editor.

- **Game:**

The Games tab contains various games that you can download to your iPad.

- **Apps:**

The application section is for non-game applications. They are arranged in categories that can be viewed.

- **Update:**

Here you can see all the updates available for the applications that are on your iPad.

- **Search:**

Use the Search tab to search for your application.
Note: You need an Apple ID and a valid credit card to purchase apps (including free apps) from the App Store.

Check out the App Store

The first time you visit the App Store, you will see a variety of new apps and games that you can check out. If you are looking for something more specific, you can press the **Apps** button to go to the category you are looking for.
Within each category you will see a list of popular applications. Each app records its price (or says **Get** if it's free). You can check the information by clicking on the app. The app page shows information about the app's behavior, user reviews, screenshots and more.

Multitasking

You may be used to using multiple programs on your computer at the same time. This is also known as multitasking. Multitasking works a little differently on the iPad. You cannot use multiple applications at one time, but you can easily switch between applications without having to go to the home screen.

To make multitasking as seamless as possible, the iPad will continue to pause recent apps in the background. If you switch to a recent app, you will not have to wait for the app to load all over again. Just pick up from where you stopped.

To switch applications

You may want to switch applications quickly without returning to the home screen. Suppose you are browsing the Internet in Safari and decide to send a message through the e-mail program.

Open the application switcher: Swipe up from the bottom edge, pause when you get to the center of the screen, and then lift your finger.

A preview of the current applications is displayed. Swipe left or right to view current applications. Just tap the app you want to open it.

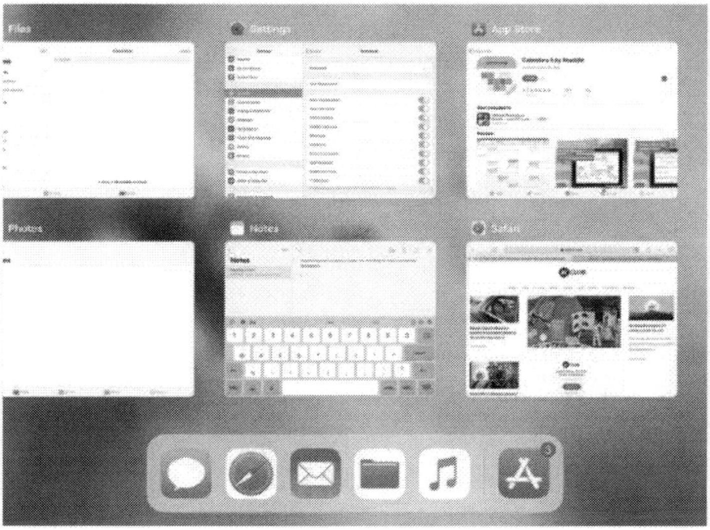

Fig 71. Swipe up to open the Application Switcher

To close the app

Even when you switch to the home screen, the app you are using does not really close. Instead, it is in standby mode in the background. However, if the app does not work properly, it may help force the app to close. This is similar to killing a program that is not responding to your computer.

Note that you do not need to close the app this way unless you are having problems. The apps are paused, so your iPad does not slow down or drain the battery.

Open the application switcher: Swipe up from the bottom edge, pause when you get to the center of the screen, and then lift your finger.

A preview of the current application is displayed. To shut down an app/program, slide it upward.

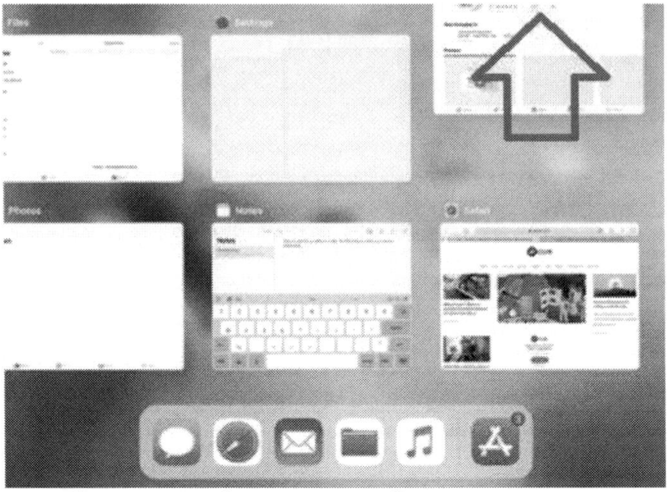

Fig 72. Swipe up to close your app

Manage applications

The home screen contains icons for all the applications in your device. This means that it can be quite crowded, especially if you have installed many apps from the App Store. Here are some tricks to customize your home screen so you can easily find your favorite apps at any time.

- To rearrange the icons, press and hold an application on the home screen. When the icon starts to shake, drag it and drop it anywhere you want (whether inside or outside the dock). To move the icon to another screen, drag the icon to the left or right edge and press and hold until you switch to a new screen. When you have finished, swipe up from the bottom of the screen to prevent the icons from shaking.

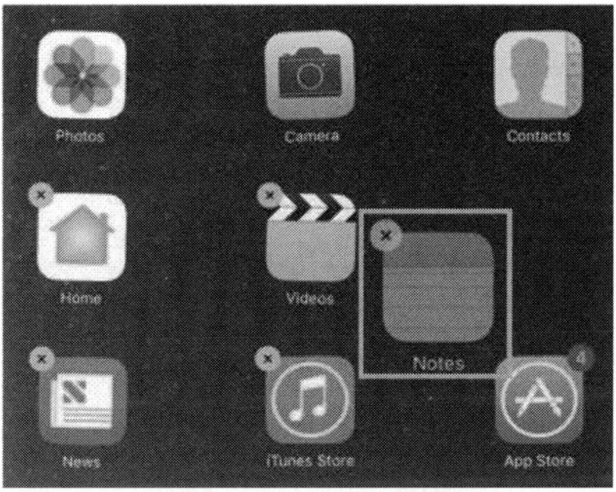

Fig 73. Press and hold. When the icon starts to shake, drag it and drop it anywhere you want.

- If you're on the last page of your app, you can drag the icon to the far right to create more home screens.

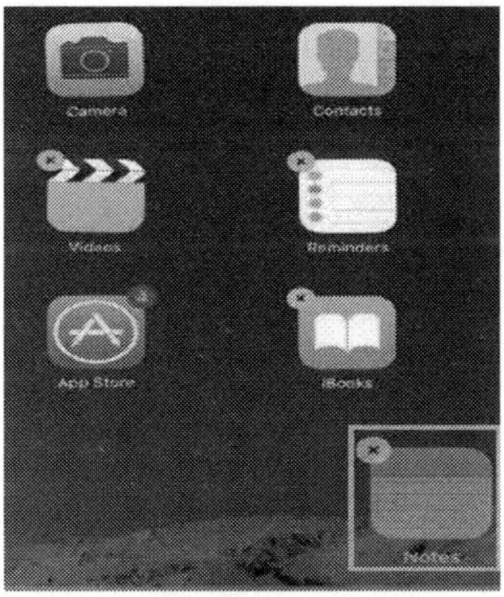

Once you finish swipe up from the bottom of the screen.

- Create a folder: Press and hold an application on the home screen. When the icon starts to shake, drag one icon to another to create a folder. Keep dragging and dropping the necessary icons to add them to the folder. This is a great way to organize similar apps and get rid of clutter from your home screen.

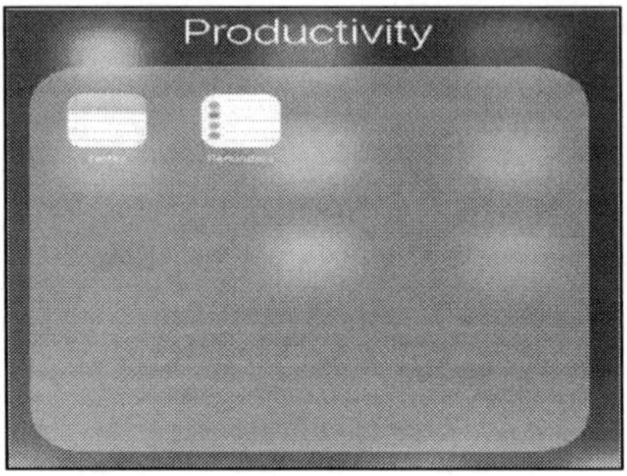

Once you finish go to the home screen. You can return to the home screen at any time by swiping from the bottom of the screen.

- Search for apps: Swipe from the middle of the Home screen to the down to find for applications. A search box will pop up at the up of the screen. When you start typing the name of the app you want, the apps that match your search will appear (along with other files and settings on the iPad).

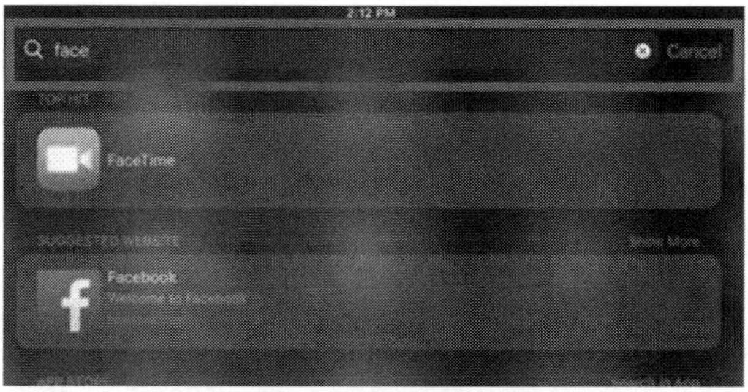

Fig 74. When you start typing the name of the app you want, the apps that match your search will appear.

- Delete apps: From your iPad's home screen, press and hold the app. When the icon starts to shake, push that X tag at it left (up).

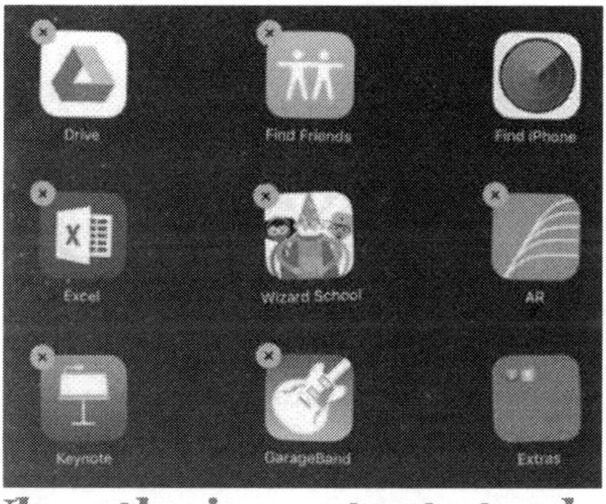

Fig 75- When the icon starts to shake, push that X tag at it left (up).

- Once you finish, swipe up from the bottom of the screen.

App updates

Over time, many applications receive updates from app developers. Updates usually help make your program smoother and can introduce new features. By default, iPad will automatically download these updates. However, you can disable this feature if you want to update the app manually. If automatic updates are turned off, a notification bar will appear on the App Store icon when updates are available for any of the installed applications.

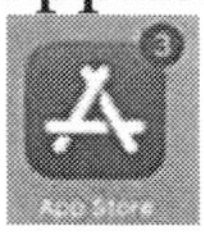

To change auto-update settings:

If desired, you can configure your ipad to install all updates automatically.

- From your iPad's home screen, press Setting 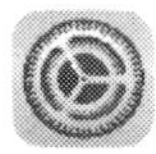 .
- Tap **iTunes & App Store**, then click **Update** to turn automatic updates on or off.

To update the application manually:

- Open the App Store.
- Then press **Updates**.
- A list of available updates is displayed.
- Press **Update** to update the application.
- You can also click on **Update all** to install all available updates.

CHAPTER 12: MAIL

Use the Mail application

Mail is probably one of the first apps you want to install on your iPad. You can use it to view and send emails, reply to messages; manage your inbox and much more that you are used to doing with your email account.

The first time you open the email application, you need to connect to your current email address. Select your email provider and follow the instructions to link your account to the email application. When done, you will be able to send and receive emails from that account on your iPad.

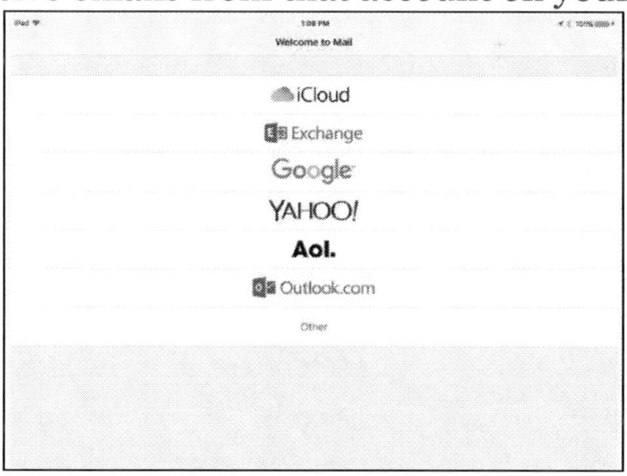

Fig 76. Select your email provider.

Add another email account

If you use multiple email accounts (for example, for personal email and for work email), you can add multiple accounts to your email application. This allows you to manage all your messages in one place.

- To add another email account, from your iPad's home screen, tap the Settings key 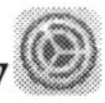.
- Tap **Mail** in the left panel.
- Tap **Accounts**.
- And then select **Add Account**.
- Do one of these:
- Click any of the email services, e.g. iCloud, Microsoft Exchange, Gmail, etc.
  Fill in the relevant email account details.
- Click **Other**.
  Press **Add Mail Account**.
  Fill in the relevant email account details.

Email notification

When you receive a new email, a sign will appear on the app icon. This number shows the number of unread emails in your inbox. This allows you to quickly search for new messages without having to open the Mail app.

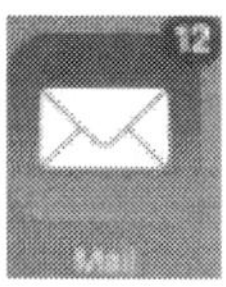

You can customize your notifications by going to Settings, clicking Notification Center, and selecting Email.

Swipe gesture

The Mail app includes some useful tools for managing your mailbox, such as folders and flags. You can also swipe left on the message to select options such as archive or delete, reply and forward.

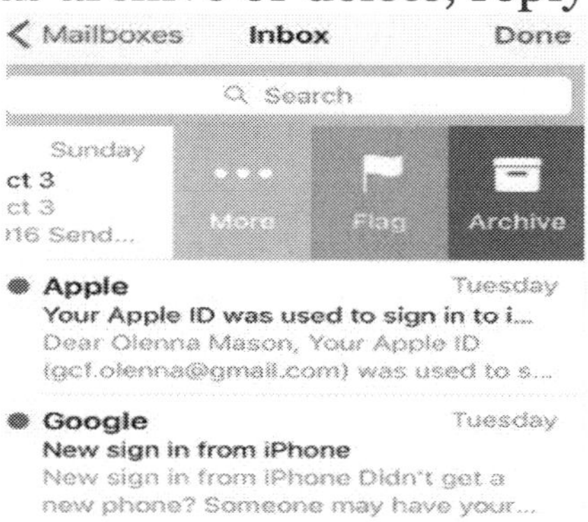

Fig 77. Swipe left on the message to select options

Customize your email signature

By default, each email you send contains the word "sent from iPad" at the bottom of the message. This is the default e-mail signature for the e-mail application. To customize or delete your email signature, do this:

tap Email in the left pane and select Signature.

- From your iPad's home screen, tap the Settings key.
- Tap **Mail** in the left panel.

- Tap **Signature**.

CHAPTER 13: CONTACTS

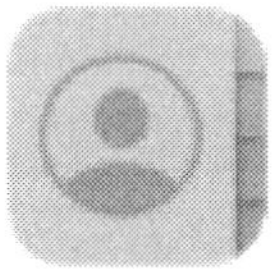

On iPad, you can use the Contacts application to save your acquaintances' contact information. You can use saved contact information to quickly call Face Time and send emails.

With the iPad, you can create as many contacts as you need, so you always have important contact information.

To add a contact:

- Click on the Contacts icon in the Home screen.
- The contacts list is displayed. Click on the + key above.

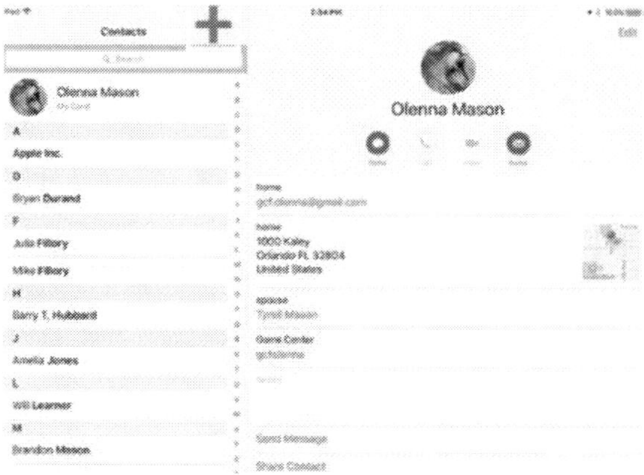

Fig 78. Click on the + key

- Enter the relevant contact information. At the very least, you need to enter the 1st and last name and email address. However, you can also enter other information such as phone number, address and birthday.

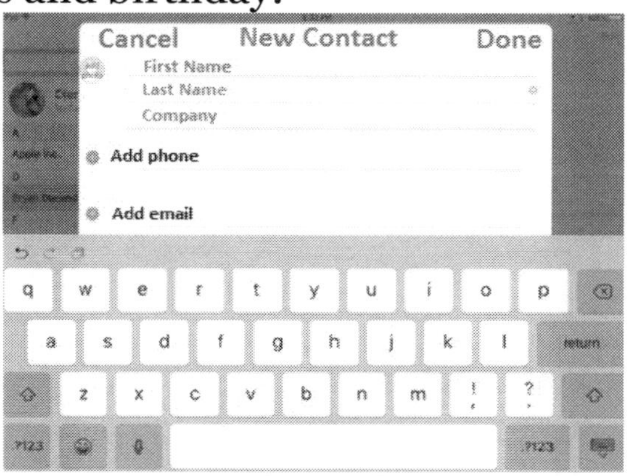

Fig 79. Enter the relevant contact information.

- When you are finished, tap **Done**.

- To edit information for an existing contact, select the contact, and tap **Edit**.

Navigating through Contacts

If you have a lot of people on your contact list, it can be difficult to find them quickly. Happily, you can quickly browse through your contacts using one of the options:

- **Search:**

You can quickly search for all your contacts by using the search bar at the top of your contacts list. Just tap the search bar and type. Contacts that match your search are displayed.

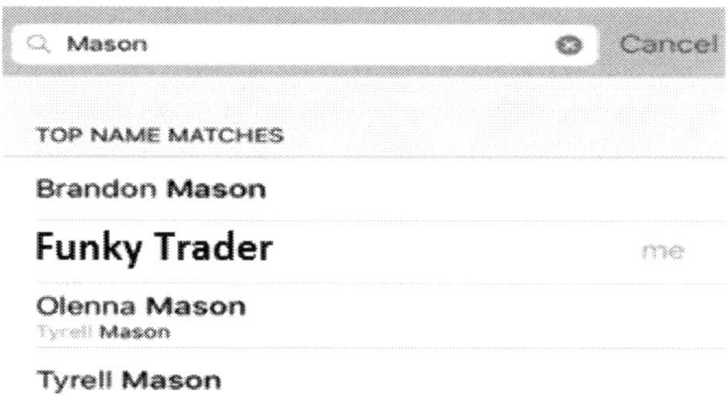

Fig 80. Using the search bar

- **Browse Letters:**

Quickly view your contact list by letter. Just tap the character you want on the right side of your contact list. You can also quickly scroll through your contacts by dragging the text up or down.

To Set Up My Info Card:

If you want Siri to have access to your personal contact information, you need to install a My Info Card. This allows Siri to respond to more complex requests, such as giving instructions to your home or reminding you when you get to work.
Before you can set up your My Info Card, you need to create a contact with your name and information.

- Click on the Contacts icon in the Home screen.
- The contacts list is displayed. Click on the + key above.
- Fill in your own Contact details. This is what will be used for creating your Card.
- Return to the home screen by swiping from the bottom of the screen.
- From your iPad's home screen, tap the Settings key .
- Scroll down and click on **Contacts** in the left panel.
- Scroll down and press **My Info** under Contacts.
- The contact list is displayed. Find and choose your name.
- Your information will be placed on My Card.

To add a relationship tag:

If you want Siri to understand your interactions with different contacts (for example, Angela is your brother and Susan is your mother), you can add a contact tag.

To add a contact tag, press and hold the top key to access Siri.
Then describe the relationship you have with your contact (e.g. Angela Jason is my brother).
Tap **Yes**.

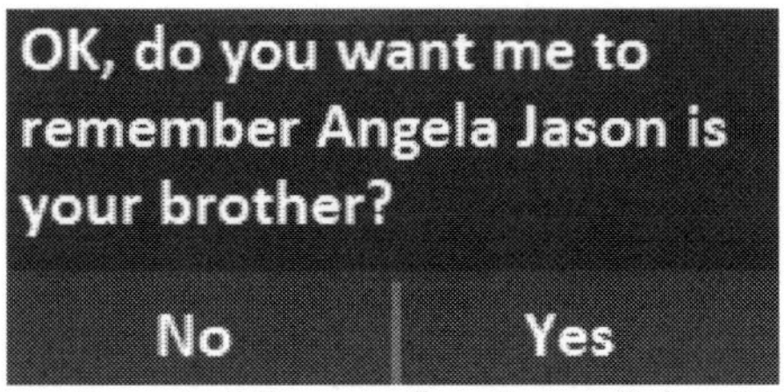

Fig 81. Add a relationship Tag

After adding a relationship, Siri can respond to personal requests, such as **Call my husband** or send a text message to my mother.
You can also set the contact tag of the contact manually. Do this:

- Click on the Contacts icon in the Home screen.
- While viewing your contacts, tap **Edit.**
- Scroll down and pick **Add related name**.
- Do one of these:
  - Type in your relationship with that person.
  - Click on the blue relationship suggested. Pick one of the available relationships.
- Tap **Done**.

CHAPTER 14: MESSAGES

Probably, one of the first things that come to your mind as far as using mobile devices is concerned is that you need to send Text Messages, isn't it? If you've been using Apple Devices for some time now, you'll likely know that the default text messaging app for Apple is the Messages app.

Text messages are sent/receive from/to the Messages app as SMS, MMS or iMessage.

The messaging app allows you to send text messages as iMessage to users with an iPhone, iPad, iPod touch or Mac via Wi-Fi. SMS and MMS messages can be sent to anybody using a Mobile device that has cellular service. Texts sent and received via iMessage do not count towards your mobile messaging plan's SMS/MMS allowance, but mobile data charges may apply.

An iMessage text can contain images, videos, and other information. See when others are posting and send read receipts to let them know you've read your messages. For security reasons, messages sent via iMessage are encrypted before they are sent.

iMessage text appears in blue speech bubbles and SMS/MMS text appears in green speech bubbles.

Signing in to iMessage

You'll have to sign in to iMessage on all your devices if you wish to use it across board.

Sign in on iPad

- Open your device's Settings app
- Scroll down and tap **Messages**.
- Switch on iMessage.

Sign in on Mac and other Apple devices with the same Apple ID

When you sign in to iMessage with the same Apple ID on all your devices, all the messages you send and receive on your iPad appear on your other Apple devices. Send a message from the next device or use Handoff to start a conversation on one device and continue on another.

Do this (for iPhone/ iPad/ iPod)

- Open your device's Settings app
- Scroll down and tap **Messages**.
- Switch on iMessage.

Do this on your Mac:

- Open Messages
- Do one of these:
  - ➢ If this is the first time you are signing, fill in your Apple ID and password. Then press **Sign In**.
  - ➢ If you have already signed in previously and will like to use a different Apple ID now, you'll need

to first sign out of the previous Apple ID, before signing in with the new one. Do this:

- Choose **Messages**.
- Press **Preferences**
- Press **iMessage**
- Now follow the whole process to sign in with the new Apple ID & Password.

Continuity lets you send and receive SMS/MMS messages on your iPad using your iPhone's cellular connection.

Using Messages in iCloud

- Open your device's Settings app
- Press your account name.
- Press iCloud
- If Messages is disabled, switch it on.

All the messages you send and receive on your iPad are stored in iCloud. And if you sign in with the same Apple ID on a new device that also has iCloud messaging enabled, all your conversations will appear there automatically.
All your messages and attachments are stored in iCloud, so you can free up space on your iPad when you need it. Notes, entire conversations, and attachments you delete from your iPad are also deleted from other Apple devices with iCloud Messaging enabled (iOS 11.4, iPadOS 13, macOS 10.13.5 and later).

Note: iCloud messages uses from your iCloud storage. When the storage gets filled, you either delete some things or upgrade to iCloud+ to get extra space.

Sending and Receiving Text Messages

Send and receive text, picture, video and voice messages with the messaging app. You can also make your messages more personal with animations, Memoji stickers, iMessage applications and more.

- To begin, swipe up to go to your device's home screen.
- Press the Messages icon

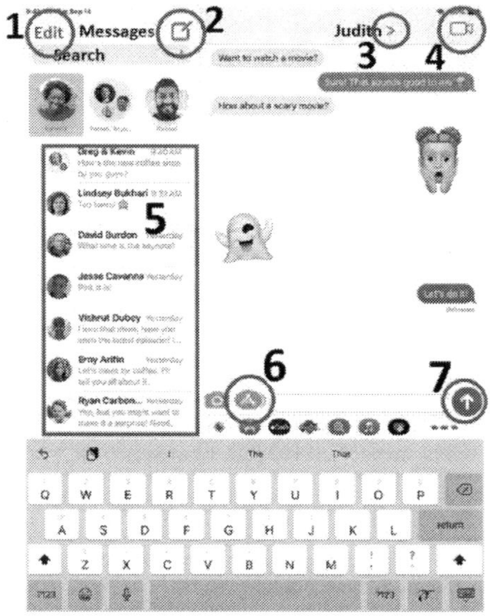

Fig 82- Messages App interface

1. *Edit Conversation List*
2. *Begin fresh conversation*
3. *Check and organize details for conversation*
4. *Switch to FaceTime call*
5. *Conversations*
6. *iMessage apps*
7. *Send message*

Send Messages

Send text messages to a single or several persons.

- Open Messages app
- To begin a fresh message thread (called conversation), press at the top of the screen.
- Or press one of the conversations that are already present.

- Fill in the name, phone number or Apple ID of each person you're sending to.
- Or press to select a contact.
- Press the text box.
- Type your message.
- Press to send.
- If the send button is blue, know that the message is going to be sent via iMessage (meaning your recipient has an apple device and that you're connected to WiFi).
- If the send button is green, know that the message is going to be sent via SMS, MMS or mobile service.
- If the message cannot be sent, a warning is displayed. Press the notification and try to send the message a second time.

To check when a message was sent or received, push the bubble for that message to the left.

- Press a name or phone number at the top of the screen to check details of your conversation. Press a contact to change the contact card, share them your location, look-up attachments, exit a group conversation, and more.

Reply to Messages

Do these:

- Open Messages app

- In the list of conversations, press any conversation you'll like to reply to.
- To find contacts and the contents that are embedded in your conversations, pull down the list of conversations and type what you're looking for in the search box. Or pick from among the contacts, links, pictures and others suggested.
- Press the text field.
- Now enter your message.

Funky-Tip: If you'll like to send emojis rather than text, do this:

- Press either or .
- Now Press each word that's highlighted.
- Press so that the message can be sent.

Here's another Funky-tip: If you want to rapidly respond to messages using quick Tapback expressions (such as thumbs-up or hearts), do this:

- Double-press the bubble of the message you're responding to.
- Now press one of the Tapback expressions.

You should definitely try it out. Bet you, your receiver will be dazzled.

Yet another Funky-tip: You can have Siri reply your messages for you. Do this:

- Say "Hey Siri" or press the top button and keep on holding it till Siri comes up.
- Say something, e.g.

"Send text message to Matthew saying How do you do?"
"Help me Read out the last message I got from Meetra"

"Reply that's wonderful"

Funky-Tip Again! If you have gotten an AirPod (2nd generation or later), an AirPod Pro, an AirPod Max, or other supported headphones, there's more Siri can do for you in Messages. For instance, while you're wearing your AirPod, it can read out messages you receive, and in turn you'll be able to say a reply and have Siri send them for you.

Pin conversations

While using the Messages app, you'll likely have messages from some people that quite very relevant, if you know what I mean. For such contacts, you can pin their conversations to the up of your Conversation list. This way, messages from them will be the first to catch your eye.

- Open Messages app
- Do one of these:
  - In the list of conversations, Swipe across any conversation you'll like to pin (swipe to the right). Now press .
  - Press the person's conversation, hold it and push it to the up of your conversation list.

Unpin Conversations

When you no longer want a conversation at the top of your list, unpin it.

- Open Messages app
- Do one of these:
- Press the pinned conversation, hold it and push it to the bottom of your conversation list.
- Press the pinned conversation, hold it and then press .

Sharing your name and picture

In the Messages app, your name & picture can be shared while you're replying or beginning fresh messages. The image can be from a Memoji you created or one of your custom images. The first time you open Messages, you'll receive iPad directions to help you pick a name and photo.
If you later want to modify your name, pictures, or other sharing options, do these:

- Open Messages app
- Press more
- Press Edit your Name & Photo
- Do one of these:
    - **Modify the profile picture**: Press Edit. Pick an option.
    - **Modify the name**: Press the text box where your name is displayed.

- **Switch on/off sharing**: Press the button beside Name and Photo Sharing (green is on).
- **Change those who can view the profile**: Press one of the options under Share Automatic. Before you can do this, you must first switch on Name & Photo Sharing.

The name & picture you're using in your Messages will also be applied to your Apple ID and in your Contacts' My Card.

Switching from a conversation in Messages app to a Video or Audio call in FaceTime

In Messages, you can start a FaceTime audio or video call with your chat partner.

- Open Messages app
- Begin a conversation
- In the conversation, press
- Press one of these:
  - FaceTime audio
  - FaceTime video

Sending Businesses Messages

Some companies let you contact them directly, ask questions, solve problems, get expert advice on what you're buying, and even buy using Apple Pay.

- Use Maps, Safari, Search or Siri to find the company you are going to chat with.

- Press the chat link in the searching results to begin a conversation.
- Chat links can look different: they may be buttons, text links or company logos.
- With some companies, you can even begin a chat straight from their websites or apps.

Funky-Tip: Messages you send to participating companies are displayed in dark gray, to differentiate them from messages you sent via iMessage (blue) and SMS/MMS (green).

Sending messages to Groups

At times, you may want to spread one message to several persons at once. Rather than going through the stress of sending each person the message, one by one, create a group conversation and send your message to the group at once. The Messages app allows you to send messages to groups. Group messages allow you to reply or call attention to a specific message.

Sending a fresh message to the group

You have to start a group conversation. This can be easily done by sending the same message to multiple people.

- Open Messages app
- Press at the up of the screen to begin your fresh conversation.

- Fill each receiver's phone number, his/her contact name, or their Apple ID; or press and then select the contacts.
- Press the text field.
- Enter your message.
- Then tap

Funky-Tip: If one or more receivers do not use iMessage, the messages you send are going to show up in a green bubble rather than a blue one.

Respond to a particular message from group messages

Reply to particular messages in groups or even individual conversations to help enhance clarity and keep your conversations well organized.

- Open Messages app
- Open one of the conversations
- In that conversation, touch the particular message you wish to respond to and hold it.
- Press
- Type what you want to reply
- Press send

Provided everyone in the group has an Apple device (iPhone, iPad, iPod touch, or Mac) whose iMessage is on, they will be able to reply in turn.

Adding persons to existing group messages

- Open Messages app
- Press that group message you'll like to add the person to.
- Press the picture of the Group by the up of the messages thread.
- Press Add Contact.
- Fill the person's phone number, his or her contact name, or their Apple ID.

Someone can only be added to a group message that already exists only if everybody in that group has an Apple device (iPhone, iPad, iPod touch, or Mac) whose iMessage is switched on). If not, you'll have to begin a fresh group message.

Removing a person from a group message

As long as there are at least three people in the thread (and everyone is on an iPhone, iPad, iPod touch, or Mac and iMessage is turned on), you can remove someone from a group message.

- Open Messages app
- Press that group message you'll like to delete the person from.
- Press the picture of the Group by the up of the messages thread.

- Swipe across the name of that person you will like to remove from your group (swipe to the left).
- Now press Remove.

If your group is too loud or rowdy, you can mute that conversation, regardless of the number of persons in this group. When you mute a group, you'll not receive notifications from that group.

Leave a group message

Tired of a particular group? You can easily leave it. But everyone in that group must have an Apple Device (iPhone, iPad, iPod, Mac) whose iMessage is on.

- Open Messages app
- Press that group message you'll like to leave.
- Press the picture of the Group by the up of the messages thread.
- Scroll down to **Leave this conversation**. Press it.

Specify persons in your group

In group messages, you can mention someone's name to draw his/her attention to a particular message. Provided everyone in that group must have an Apple Device (iPhone, iPad, iPod, Mac) whose iMessage is on, they are going to be notified. Based on their individual settings, they'll receive the notice, whether they've muted the group or not.

- Open Messages app
- Open the group conversation
- Start to type the name of that person in the text field.
- When the name of that contact comes up, press it.
- Another way you can specify a person is to type @ and then the person's name.

If you wish to set your personal notification preferences for when someone mentions you in a group message, do this:

- Swipe up to return to your device's home screen
- Open Settings app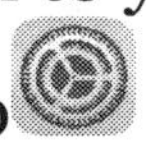
- Press **Messages**
- Press **Notify Me**.

Change the message name and picture for your group

You can attach a individualized name or photo to a group conversation. Again, everyone in that group must have an Apple Device (iPhone, iPad, iPod, Mac) whose iMessage is on.

- Open Messages app
- Press that group message you'll like to change its name/picture.
- Press the name/number by the up of that conversation.
- Press **Change Name & Photo**.
- Pick an item.

CHAPTER 15: PHONE CALLS

iPhones are wonderful devices for making phone calls. On iPads, the process is a little tricky. Phone calls can be made on iPads using WiFi Calling. What happens is that the phone call gets relayed to the iPad via your iPhone. So you must have an iPhone (having at least iOS 9) and good WiFi connection to make phone calls from your iPad.

You may receive Mobile charges. Not all carriers support Wi-Fi calling.

Take Note: If you have a Wi-Fi + Cellular model, your iPad cannot handle Cellular phone service. It only uses Cellular Data transmission.

Before you start

Do these:

- Set FaceTime up on both iPhone and iPad.
- Use the same Apple ID to sign in to the two devices.

Allow iPad phone calls from the iPhone

You're going to need to set up the iPhone first, before moving on to the iPad.

Do these on your iPhone:

- Open Settings app
- Press **Cellular**
- If there are two SIMs in the iPhone, pick one of them (under Cellular Plans).

- Do one of these:
  - Press **Calls on other devices**
    Activate **Allow Call on Other Device**
    Now choose iPad, plus every other device from which you'll want to make the phone calls from and also receive them.
    This allows you to make and answer calls when an iPad or other device associated with the same Apple ID is near your iPhone and has Wi-Fi connection.
  - Press Wi-Fi Calling.
    Switch on **Add WiFi Callings on Other Device**.
    This one is going to allow you to make and answer calls on your iPad or other device connected to the same Apple ID, even if your iPhone isn't nearby.

Do these on your iPad:

- Open Settings app
- Press **FaceTime**
- Activate **FaceTime & Calls from iPhone** (green is on)
- When prompted, Switch on **WiFi Callings**.

Now you're ready.
Once you're done setting up Wi-Fi calling on both your iPhone and iPad, you will be able to make and answer phone calls from your iPad.

Make a Call

- Swipe up to return to your device's home screen

- Go to any app that contains the phone number of a person you want to call (Contacts app, Calendar app, FaceTime, Messages, Search, Safari, etc.)
- Press the phone number.
- Press

Answer a call

When you're called, a notice pops up.

If you wish to Answer or ignore that call, slide or press the notification.

Please Note: Once Wi-Fi Calling is turned on and there's an emergency, they can use your iPad to make emergency calls over WiFi, regardless of whether location services are turned on or not. Also, and your device's location may be used to direct those who will help you.

Additional some carriers can use the address you registered with them as your location when you signed up for Wi-Fi calling.

CHAPTER 16: SET UP FACETIME

The popularity of video calling has increased in recent years and it is a really good way to keep in touch with each other when we aren't able to see our loved ones physically. Apple has its own video calling program called FaceTime, and it's built into almost every Apple device, including your favorite iPad. Whether you're using an iPhone, iPad, iPod touch, or Mac, you can use the FaceTime app to stay in touch with your friends and family. With internet connection, you are just a few taps away to see and connect with your loved ones.

With a feature called **Spatial Audio** in FaceTime, the people you're talking to will sound like they're in the same room as you, speaking from their screen position. This spatial audio feature works with AirPods (3rd generation and later), AirPods Pro (all generations), and AirPods Max (sold separately).

With another apple feature, **SharePlay**, you can watch movies and TV shows together, or listen to music together during a FaceTime call. You can share your screen, browse apps, websites and more during a call. Collaborate on documents, view photo albums, plan your next group vacation, and get feedback on what you're working on. Listen to other people's responses during a call.

Use the front camera to talk face-to-face or switch to the rear camera to share what you see around you, like what you're cooking, what's on your table, your beautiful painting, and the likes. To capture moments of conversation, take a FaceTime Live photo.

Something else! Before now, you could only have a FaceTime call to fellow Apple users. Well that's come to an end. With the web version, even none Apple users can enjoy all the exciting goodness FaceTime has to offer. Get ready! We're taking your FaceTime experience to a whole new level.

We'll learn how you can harvest all these cool FaceTime features in this chapter. To begin, do this:

- Open your iPad's Settings
- Scroll down till you find **FaceTime**. Click it.
- Switch on FaceTime (green).
- Press **Use Apple ID for FaceTime**.
- Fill in the Apple ID and the password for your account.
- Click **Sign In**.

Note: If you don't have an Apple ID, you can create one now.

- Once you're sure FaceTime is turned on, then do one of these:
    - Click **SharePlay**, then switch on SharePlay: This will enable you to Watch TV shows and

movies together, listen to music together and share your screen in conversations during your FaceTime call.
- o Switch on **Speaking**: This is going to highlight the person that's speaking in a conversation on Facetime:
- o Switch on **Live Captions**: This is going to transcribe and show real-time text during conversations on FaceTime. Please let everyone in the conversation know that their speech is being transcribed on their device. Note: At the time of writing, this feature was in beta.
- o Switch on **FaceTime Live Photos**: This will enable you to take live photos during FaceTime calls.
- o Switch on **Eye Contact**: This establishes natural eye contacts during FaceTime calls

Get a link to FaceTime call

Have you ever wanted to make a FaceTime call to a friend who doesn't have an iPad or some other Apple device? How did you do it? Is it even possible? Yes!

With the FaceTime app, you can create a link to your FaceTime call and send it to your friends or groups (via email or message). From their end, they can use the link to join or start a conversation/call.

- Open your FaceTime app.
- Press **Create Link** by the top of your iPad.

- Choose an option to send the link (email, message, etc.).

In the Calendar app, you can schedule remote video meetings by adding FaceTime as a meeting location.
Note: You can invite anyone to join your FaceTime call, even if they don't have an Apple device. They can join one-on-one and group FaceTime calls from their browser (e.g. Google Chrome or Microsoft Edge). No login required.
Simply follow the above steps to create a FaceTime link, send it to your friend, let them click on it or copy and paste it in their browser and you guys can instantly start your call. (Note: FaceTime via browser requires the latest version of Chrome or Edge. You'll need a special video encoding language (H.264) to send videos).

Make and receive FaceTime calls

With an internet connection and an Apple ID, you can make and receive calls using the FaceTime app.
Note: FaceTime must be set up to make and answer calls.
You can also make FaceTime calls through your mobile data connection, but additional charges may apply. To disable this feature, do this:

- Open your iPad's Settings
- Scroll down till you find **Mobile**. Click it.
- Switch off **FaceTime**.

Call on FaceTime

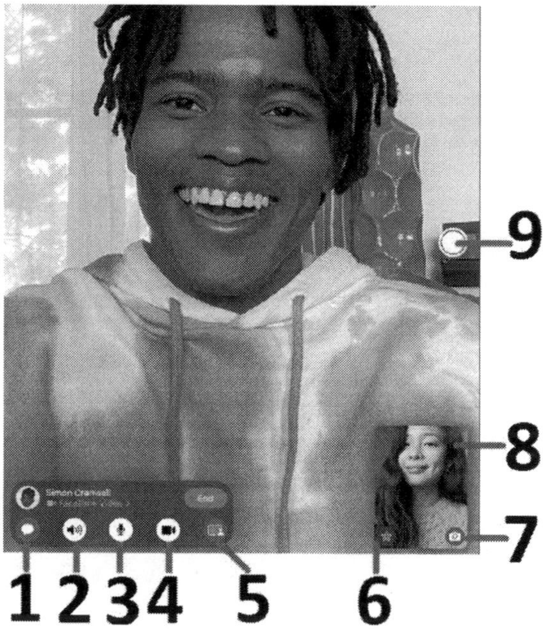

Fig 83: One-on-one FaceTime call

1. *Send a Message*
2. *Loudspeaker*
3. *Mute your mic*
4. *Switch off your camera*
5. *SharePlay*
6. *Insert stickers & other exciting effects*
7. *Change to the rear camera*
8. *Pull your image to one corner*
9. *Take Live Photos*

Funky-Tip: You can use Siri to open the FaceTime app. Stay within audible range from the iPad. Then say "Hey Siri!" just loud enough **For You**r iPad or iPhone to hear your voice. Now Say, "Make a FaceTime call."

- In FaceTime, click **New FaceTime** near the top of the screen.
- Enter the name or number you want to call in the top entry field.
- Click to make a video call.
- Click to make a voice call.

(Not available in all countries/regions).

Alternatively, you can click the green plus to open your contacts and add people from there.
Or click a suggested contact in your call history to make a quick call.
Funky-Tip: To see more during a FaceTime video call, rotate your iPad to landscape mode.
If your iPad's screen orientation lock is on, this will not work. When it's locked, you'll see the lock screen icon on the status bar at the top of your screen. To turn off the screen orientation lock, swipe downward from the right-top side of the screen. This will open the Control Center. Click the icon for Lock screen.

Receive FaceTime Calls

When you get a FaceTime call, do one of the following:

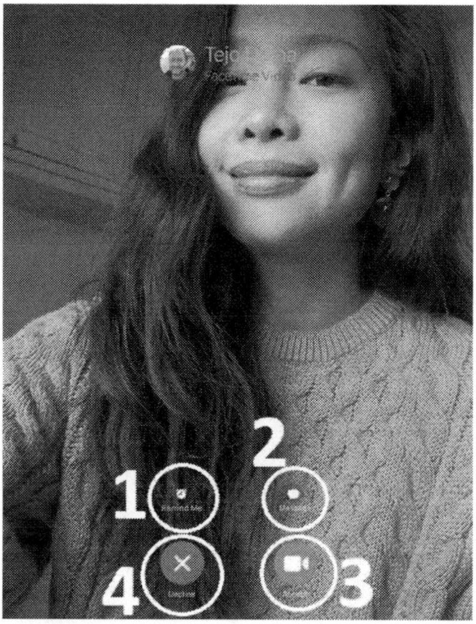

*Fig 84. **Receive One-on-One FaceTime Calls***

1. *Set a callback reminder: Click **Remind Me** to set a Reminder to call the Caller back at a later time.*
2. *Send a text message to the caller: Click **Message** to send a text message to the person calling you.*
3. *Answer the call: Drag the slider or click **Accept**.*
4. *Reject the call: Click **Decline**.*

If you're on another call when a FaceTime call comes in, you'll see the **End and Accept** option instead of **Accept**. This ends the previous call and connects you to the received call.

Tip: You can request Siri to proclaim incoming calls. That way you can accept or reject calls by voice.

Begin a FaceTime Audio/Video call from Messages

In a messaging conversation, you can start a FaceTime conversation with your chat partner.

- Click 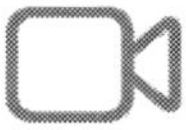 in the upper right corner of the message conversation.
- Do one of the following:
    - Click **FaceTime Audio**.
    - Click **FaceTime Video**.

Leave a message

When you call someone in FaceTime and no one answers your FaceTime call, you can do one of the following:

- Click Leave a message.
- Click Cancel.
- Click Call Back.

Call back

In your call history, click on the name or number of the person (or group) you want to call back.

Delete a call from your call history

In FaceTime, swipe left on the conversation in your call history.
Now click **Delete**.

Take Live Photos

During a video call with the FaceTime app, you can take a FaceTime Live Photo to capture moments of conversation (not available in all countries/regions). The camera captures what happened just before and after the shot, including sound, so you can see and hear exactly what happened afterwards.

Before attempting to shoot a FaceTime Live photo, ensure FaceTime Live Photos is active. Do this:

- Open your iPad's Settings
- Scroll down till you find **FaceTime**. Click it.
- Check if **FaceTime Live Photos** is on (green is on). If it's not, turn it on.
- Now Open your FaceTime app.
- Then do one of these:
    - In a one-on-one FaceTime Call, click the shutter.
    - During a group FaceTime call: Click the panel for the person you want to take a photo of, click , then click.

Both you and the person will receive a notification that the photo has been taken and a live image will be saved in the Photos app on your iPad.

Turn on Live Captions for FaceTime calls

When you're on a video call with the FaceTime app, you can turn on Live Text (beta) to see the call transcribed on your screen. Live Text converts spoken words into written text and displays it on your iPad's screen during a Call. If conversations are hard to hear, live captions can help.

In high-risk circumstances, please do not rely on Live Captions, as their accuracy may sometimes vary. Live Caption consumes extra battery.

Note: Live Captions is currently in beta.

- During a FaceTime video call, click the screen to display FaceTime controls (if not visible).
- Click ⓘ at the top of the controls to turn on real-time text, then click **Done**.
- A Live Caption dialog will appear, automatically displaying the transcribed dialogue of the conversation at the top of the screen and who is speaking.

To stop showing the transcribed dialogue on your screen, do this:

- Click the screen to display FaceTime controls (if not visible).
- Click ⓘ the top of the FaceTime controls
- Then turn off Live Captions.

Using other apps during FaceTime calls

While on a call with the FaceTime app, you can use other apps to look up information or do calculations.

- Swipe upward from the bottom of screen. You're going to be taken to the home screen.
- Click the icon of the app you want to use (e.g. Calculator, Calendar, etc.) to open the app.
- To return to the FaceTime screen, click the green bar (or the FaceTime icon) at the top of the screen.

CHAPTER 17: MAKE GROUP FACETIME CALLS

The FaceTime app allows you to include up to 32 participants in a group FaceTime call (not available in all countries/regions).

Start a group FaceTime call

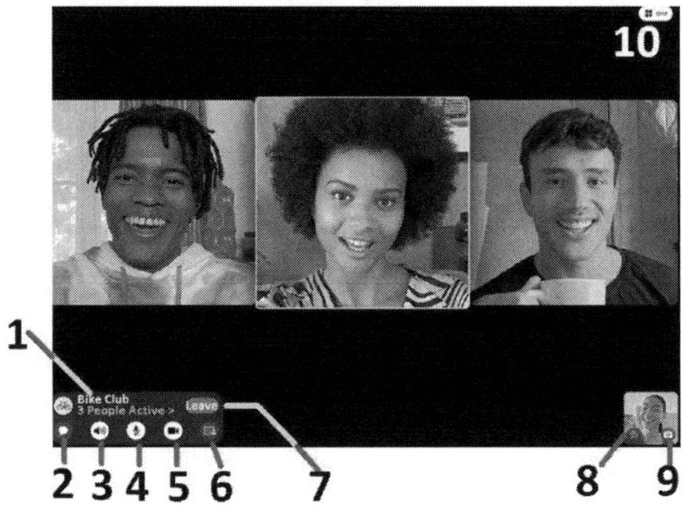

Fig 85. Group FaceTime call

1. *Add new participants*
2. *Send a Message*
3. *Loudspeaker*
4. *Mute your mic*
5. *Switch off your camera*
6. *SharePlay*
7. *Leave group call*
8. *Insert stickers & other exciting effects*
9. *Change to the rear camera*
10. *View Participants in a Grid*

- Open your FaceTime app.
- In FaceTime, click **New FaceTime** near the top of the screen.
- Enter the name or number of the person you want to call in the typing field above.
- You can also click the green plus to open your contacts and add people from there. Alternatively, click a contact suggested from your call history.
- Click to make a video call
- Click to send a Voice call.

Each participant is represented by tiles on the screen. When a participant speaks (verbally or signs) or clicks a tile, the tile is identified. Tiles that do not fit the screen appear side by side below. Swipe continuously to find participants teachers who are missing (participants' initials may appear on tiles if photos are not available).

If you don't want the speaker or signer tile to become larger during a group FaceTime call, do this:

- Open your iPad's Settings
- Scroll down till you find **FaceTime**. Click it.
- Below the heading Automatic Prominence, switch off **Speaking** (green is on).

Note: If your device is recent, it may be able to detect Sign language. Additionally, both the person presenting and the attendees will need to have at least iOS 14, iPadOS 14, macOS 11 or later.

Start a group FaceTime call from a group Message chat

Group Messaging lets you start a group FaceTime conversation with anyone you're chatting with in Messages.

- To begin, send someone a message to begin a Messages conversation.
- Click in the upper right corner of the message conversation.
- Do one of the following:
  - Click FaceTime Audio.
  - Click FaceTime Video.

Add another person to the conversation

Participants can add other persons at any time during the FaceTime call.
During a FaceTime call, click the screen to display the FaceTime controls (if they're not visible).

Click ⓘ at the top of the controls, and then click **Add People**.
Enter the name, Apple ID or phone number of the person you want to add in the entry field above.

Or click the green plus sign ⊕ to add someone from your contacts.
Click **Add People**.

Join a Group FaceTime call

When someone invites you to join a group FaceTime call, you'll receive a call notification. You can participate or decline.

Leave a group FaceTime call

Click **Leave** to leave the group conversation at any time.
If two or more participants remain in a call, the conversation continues. If not, the call ends automatically.

Show participants in a grid

When you're in a conversation with 4 or more people in the FaceTime app, you can see the participants in equal-sized tiles arranged in a grid. Speaker tiles are automatically highlighted so you can easily see who is speaking. (Depending on the iPad model, the tiles may appear blurry.)
In a FaceTime call, click the **Grid** button (it's in the bottom-left of your screen). If you don't see the button, click your screen.
Click the **Grid** button again to turn off the Grid layout.

How to Use SharePlay in FaceTime

SharePlay in FaceTime app lets you stream TV shows, movies and music in sync with friends and family during FaceTime calls. Enjoy real-time connection with other users in conversation. Synchronized playback and shared controls let you see and hear the same moment at the same time. With smart volume, Audio is dynamically adjusted so you can keep chatting while you watch and listen. SharePlay can also be used with other apps during FaceTime calls. To see which apps are available for SharePlay during a call, click  and scroll through the apps under SharePlay Apps.

Note: You may need a subscription to utilize some applications that support SharePlay. To watch a movie or TV show together, each participant must have a device that meets the minimum system requirements and have access to content on their own device through subscription or purchase. SharePlay may not support sharing of certain movies or TV shows in different countries or regions. In some countries or geo-regions, certain features in FaceTime, as well as some services of Apple, aren't accessible.

Watching videos together

You can watch movies and TV shows during FaceTime calls with friends and family.

- Start a FaceTime call.
- Go to your home screen (swipe upward from the bottom of the iPad's screen).
- Open a video streaming app that supports SharePlay (like the Apple TV app).
- Select the show or movie you want to watch, click the **Play** button
- Then choose **Play with Everyone** (if available) to start watching with everyone in the conversation. (Others in the conversation may need to press **Join SharePlay** to see the video.)
- The video will start playing simultaneously for all conversation participants who have access to the content. Users without access will be prompted for access (via subscription, contract, or free trial, if available).

Anyone watching your content can use the playback controls to play, pause, rewind, and fast forward. (Each person controls settings such as closed Caption and Volume individually.)

Picture-in-picture allows you to continue watching videos while using another application. If you don't want to be interrupted by the sound of a movie, you can order food, check your email, or jump into the Messages app to discuss video over text.

Invite friends to watch videos together from supported apps during a FaceTime call

On iPad (& other Apple devices that meet the minimum system requirements), while browsing or watching video, start a FaceTime call in the Apple TV app (or another supported video app) and use SharePlay to connect with others. You can share things synchronously. All conversation participants must be able to access the content on their devices (for example through subscription or purchase).

- Open a video streaming app that supports SharePlay (like the Apple TV app tv).
- After opening you Apple TV app (or any other application you're using to stream videos), find a show or the movie you want to share and click the item to view details.
- Click, and then click SharePlay.
- In the **To** field, enter the contact you want to share with and click FaceTime.
- Once the FaceTime call is connected, click **Start** or **Play** to start using SharePlay.
- To start watching, the recipient clicks **Open**.

Note: If content requires a subscription, non-subscribers may need to subscribe before viewing.

Once the video starts playing, you can stream it to your Apple TV.

Cast what you're watching on SharePlay to your Apple TV

If you've already started watching a video together on your iPad, you can send it to your Apple TV and enjoy it on the big screen.

Do one of these:

- In the streaming app, click
  Now select **Apple TV** as the playback destination.
- Open Control Center (swipe downward from the top-right of the screen
  Click and select **Apple TV** for playback.

Videos play in sync on your Apple TV, and you can continue the conversation on your iPad.

Listening to music together

Meet others and listen to your albums and favorite playlists through FaceTime calls. Any conversation participant who has access to music (via subscription, offer, free trial, etc.) on a device that meets the minimum system requirements can listen to music, see what's next, and add songs to the shared queue.

- Start a FaceTime group call.
- Go to your home screen (swipe upward from the bottom of your iPad's screen).

- Open a music streaming app that supports SharePlay (like the Music app).
- Select the music you want to listen to and press the **Play** button to start a playlist tailored to the music. (Others in the conversation may need to press **Join SharePlay** to hear the music.)
- The music will start playing simultaneously for all conversation participants who have access to the content. Users without access will be prompted for access (via subscription, contract, or free trial, if available).

Anyone can use the music controls to pause, rewind, fast forward, skip to another part of the song, or go to the next song. Also, anyone in the conversation can add songs to the shared queue.

Invite friends to listen to music together from supported apps during a FaceTime call

On iPad (& other Apple devices that meet the minimum system requirements), you can make a FaceTime call in the Music app (or another supported music app) and use SharePlay to sync and share music with others in the conversation. Anyone can use the music controls to pause, rewind, fast forward and skip to another part of the song. Also, anyone using SharePlay can add songs to the shared queue. People you want to share with must have access to your music (for example, through a subscription).

- Open the Apple Music app (or another simple music app) and click the music you want to share.
- Do one of the following:
  - Click **More** (three dots) next to Music, and then click **SharePlay**.
  - In the upper right corner, click **More** (three dots), press and then press **SharePlay**.
- In the **To** field, enter the contact you want to share with and click **FaceTime**.
- After the FaceTime call connects, click **Start**.
- To start listening, the recipient clicks the song title at the top of the FaceTime controls, and then clicks **Open**. The music starts playing at the same time for everyone in the conversation who can access the content.

Note: People who don't have access to the content you share will be prompted to do so.
Using Shareplay, you can also share your screen to show apps, websites and more during a call.

Sharing your screen During a FaceTime call

The FaceTime app lets you share your screen in a FaceTime call and bring apps, websites, and more into the conversation. Get feedback on what you're working on, collaborate on a document, show off your photo album, plan your next vacation together, and see what others are doing in your visible and audible conversations.

Start sharing your screen

During a FaceTime group call, click the screen to reveal the controls (if the controls aren't visible).

Click the Share icon
Then click Share My Screen.
Do one of these:
Start sharing your screen: Under the SharePlay apps, click an app.
Display an app or document: Swipe upward to go to your home screen. Then open the app you want to share in a conversation.

You're going to see a countdown from 3 to 1 on and your screen will appear in the FaceTime call for everyone to see.

Click to stop sharing your screen.

Transfer FaceTime calls to another device

During a call in the FaceTime app, you can transfer the call to another device signed in with the same Apple ID.
Note: Ensure the contact information for the call on both devices is the same. To set your contact info, do this:

- Open your settings app
- Click on FaceTime
- Under the heading, You Can Be Reached At, choose you contact information. Do the same for both devices.

Now to transfer your FaceTime call, do this:

- Ensure the second device is on.
- Click the screen showing the call.
- A notification of the call will appear on your other device with the suggestion to "Move/Transfer the call to this [device]".
- Click the notification to transfer the call, or click in the upper right corner of the screen, then click the green.
- You'll see a preview of the call that shows your camera, microphone, and audio settings.
- Make sure the camera, microphone and audio settings are correct and click.
- You call will now go to the new device. On your original device, you will see a banner confirming that the call has been resumed elsewhere. You'll

also see the green Switch. You can press it to take the call back to the first device.

CHAPTER 18: FACETIME SETTINGS

Change FaceTime video settings

During a FaceTime call, you can turn portrait on or off, turn on the camera, or turn the camera on or off.

Blur the background using portrait mode

On iPad & other supported models, you can turn on Portrait Mode, which automatically blurs the background and brings visual focus in, just like Portrait Mode in the Camera app.

- Click your own tile during a FaceTime call.
- To switch on portrait mode, click on your tile.
- Click again to turn off portrait mode.

While on your call, you can also enable portrait mode in Control Center. Swipe downward from the top right of your screen. This will open the Control Center. Click **Video Effects**.

Switch to rear camera

- Click your own tile during a FaceTime call.

- To switch to rear camera, click on your tile.
- Click again to return back to front camera.

*When using the rear camera, press **1x** to zoom in and press again to return to original size.

Activate Center Stage

With FaceTime Center Stage, your iPad will automatically keep adjusting its front camera so as to frame while you're moving around its field of view.

- While your FaceTime call is going, swipe down from the top right corner of the home screen to access the control panel.
- Press Video Effects
- Press Center Stage and switch it on.
- To disable Center Stage, press it again.

On some iPads, you may see on your tile. Simply press your tile, and then push the icon to activate Center Stage.

Turn off the camera

During a FaceTime call, click the screen to display the controls, and then click to switch off the camera. (Click again to restart the camera.)

Change FaceTime audio settings

Spatial audio in the FaceTime app makes your friends sound as if they were in the same room as you. Their voices are well spread out and seem to come from the direction each one is positioned on the screen.

Note: This feature Audio is available on supported models and works with AirPods (2nd generation and later), AirPods Pro, and AirPods Max (sold separately).

Filter background noise

If you want to hear yourself clearly and filter out other sounds during FaceTime calls, you can activate Voice Isolation Mode (available on supported models). This mode prioritizes your voice during FaceTime calls and blocks out background noise.

- During a FaceTime call, swipe down from the top right. This will open Control Center.
- Click **Mic Mode**.
- Choose **Voice Isolation**.

Include Background sounds

If you want to hear your voice and everything around you during FaceTime calls, you can turn on wide-spectrum mode (available on supported models).

- During a FaceTime call, swipe down from the top right. This will open Control Center.
- Click Mic Mode.

- Choose **Wide Spectrum**.

Mute the Sound

During a FaceTime call, click the screen to display the FaceTime controls (if they're not visible).

Click the Mic icon to turn off the sound.

Press the Mic icon again to turn the sound back on.
If your sound is muted, your microphone will detect if you are speaking and you will be notified that the microphone is muted. You can click to unmute.

Adding Filter effects to FaceTime calls

You can become your favorite Memoji or Memoji character in a video call with the FaceTime app (for iPad with Face ID). On supported models, you can use built-in filters to change their appearance, add stickers, labels, and shapes. You can take screenshots with FaceTime that include special camera effects to add to your conversations.

Become a Memoji

In Messages on an iPad with Face ID, you can create Memoji characters to use in FaceTime calls. iPad captures your movements, facial expressions and voice and transmits them through your character.

(You Memoji character mimic you even if you bring your tongue out!)

- During a FaceTime call, click . (Click the screen if you can't see it.)
- Click
- Then pick a Memoji character (swipe between characters at the bottom, then click a character).
- Other callers will hear what you're saying, but will see your talking emoji.

Use Filters to alter your appearance

- While on a FaceTime video call, click your tile.
- Then click (supported models).
- Press to access Filters.
- Click the filters at the bottom to choose a one (swipe left or right to preview).

Add a text label

- During a call, click the screen.
- Then click
- Click the text icon Aa, then click a text label.
- To see more text label options, swipe up at the up of the text window.
- Once the label is selected, enter the text you want to appear on the label and click away from the label.
- Drag your label to where you want to it to be.

- To remove a tag, click it, then click remove ⊗.

Add stickers

- While on a FaceTime video call, click your tile.
- Then click (supported models).
- Now do one of these:
    - Click to add Memoji stickers
    - Click to add Emoji stickers
    - Click Aa, swipe up, then click .
- Click a sticker to add it to the conversation.
- Swipe left or swipe up for more options.
- Drag the sticker and place it wherever you want.
- To remove a sticker, click it, then click ⊗.

Add Shapes

- While on a FaceTime video call, click your tile.
- Then click (supported models).
- Click the shapes icon
- Then click a shape to add it to your conversation.
- Swipe up from the top of the shapes screen to see more options.
- Push the shape to the site where you desire it to be.
- To delete a shape, click it, and then click ⊗.

End the FaceTime call or Switch over to Messages

You can always end the conversation in the FaceTime app or move the conversation to Messages.

Leave a FaceTime call

Click the screen to display the FaceTime controls (if they're not visible), then click .

Switch over to Messages

To jump to a message thread everyone is chatting with, click the screen to reveal the FaceTime controls (if they're not visible).

Click at the top of the controls.

Then click Message or .

Block unwanted FaceTime calls

The FaceTime app can block FaceTime calls from unwanted callers.

- Open your FaceTime call history.
- In your FaceTime call history, click next to the contact's name, phone number, or email address you want to block.
- Scroll through till you find **Block this contact.** Click it.

- Then click **Block Contact**.
- Now pick the Contacts which you'll like to block. If you want to unblock someone you blocked, do this:
- In your FaceTime call history, click next to the contact's name, phone number, or email address you want to block.
- Scroll down and click **Unblock this contact**

CHAPTER 19: HOW TO PRINT OUT FROM IPAD

Trying to print something directly from your iPhone or iPad can be a little tricky. You might find it more convenient to send it to your email and print it from your desktop. Rest assured that printing from your mobile iPad is getting easier every year.

HIGHLIGHTS

- How to print using Apple AirPrint
- How to print by email
- How to print with other software
- Printing with Google Cloud Print

WHAT DO YOU NEED

- Apple iPhone or iPad
- Printer
- Appropriate application or software

This chapter will walk you through the process of printing from your iPhone or iPad using several different methods that suit your needs.

How to print using Apple AirPrint

AirPrint-enabled applications let you create and print high-quality documents and graphics without installing drivers or configuring print queues. The requirements are not high. Simply get your iPad (any model), iPhone 14, an iPhone 3GS or newer iPhone models, or 3rd generation iPod Touch, along

with the latest version of iOS and an AirPrint-enabled printer with the latest firmware.
Various printing devices including popular models from Canon, Epson, HP, Samsung, Brother and many other manufacturers support AirPrint (trust me; there is a high chance that your printer supports Airprint. Just check it out.). AirPrint functionality is the same for all iPad models, making it easy to use the software whether you have an a first generation iPad or 10th generation iPad- with AirPrint you can connect and print from your printer as long as both devices work connected to the same Wi-Fi network.
Because AirPrint runs on Wi-Fi, you must make sure the printer is connected to a Wi-Fi network before proceeding. Your printer will provide you with step-by-step instructions for connecting your device to your home Wi-Fi network - follow these steps first.

STEP 1: CONNECT TO WI-FI

Because AirPrint runs on Wi-Fi, you must make sure the printer and your iPad are connected to the same WiFi network before proceeding. Note that there may be multiple networks available in Office Mode and you may need to enable the AirPrint feature depending on the printer you are using. For detailed instructions on how to enable the feature and connect to Wi-Fi, refer to your printer's manual or manufacturer's website.

STEP 2: CHOOSE A PRINTER

Open an AirPrint-enabled application such as Mail, Safari, or Evernote to test the connection between your iPad and printer. Most apps have a familiar arrow (it looks like email forwarding and reply icons). Tap the icon and select **Print**, and your printer should appear as the default device selected. Otherwise, tap **Select Printer** at the top to let your iPad search for nearby printers.

STEP 3: CHOOSE NUMBER OF COPIES

Tap the **plus** and **minus** arrows to the right of Copies to select the number of copies to print. At least one copy is required, but you can print up to a total of 99 pages at a time if you'd like. You can also tap **Options** to see color options and which page to print if you have multiple pages.

STEP 4: PRINT

Once you have selected your printer and number of pages you want, click Print in the upper right corner of the page. You can cancel a print job or check its status by double-clicking the Home button, selecting Print Center in the app switcher, and clicking Cancel Print.

How to print via email

Did you think that only people had email addresses? Many newer Epson and HP models include HP ePrint or Epson Email Print, which lets you send images or documents to the email address assigned to your printer. You can print from anywhere in the world by simply emailing your files. Once set up, the process is relatively straightforward and simple, allowing you to email from your iPad. All you need to do is send an email to a compatible printer. This is obviously not an option for all users and printer models, but it is available for many models: Epson Expression and WorkForce series, new HP printers, and more.

STEP 1: ENABLE EMAIL PRINTING

If you have an email-enabled printer, turn on the email function first. The activation process varies by device. For example, an Epson user must activate his Epson Connect, but the entire process should be detailed in the printer's manual or the manufacturer's website. Your printer is assigned a default email address when it starts up (which probably corresponds to a random string of characters for a particular domain name), but you can later change this to something you actually remember. It doesn't have to be on the same wireless network as the printer. To use email printing, the printer must be connected via Wi-Fi instead of a regular USB cable.

STEP 2: PRINT

If set up correctly, simply email a document or photo from your iPad to the printer and it will automatically print the file according to your default specifications. Your printer may not accept all file formats, but it should be able to handle files such as JPEG, GIF, and PNG, as well as Word, PowerPoint, and Excel files. You can check the number of print attachments that can be included in the email from your printer manual.

How to print with other software

If neither AirPrint nor printing to email are viable options, you can obtain software directly from your printer manufacturer or other third-party sources. We recommend using Presto (formerly FingerPrint) to download a free iOS app compatible with almost any printer. The app is also available for Android and Chrome. It works by connecting your printer and computer to a third-party device, as long as both are on the same Wi-Fi network.

Alternatively, you can use the printer manufacturer's free proprietary software, such as Epson iPrint or Brother iPrint&Scan. However, many printers do not support printing software, and many printer companies do not create programs to manage their printers.

STEP 1: DOWNLOAD AND INSTALL THE APP

Once you've decided on an app, visit the manufacturer's website or the app's appropriate page on the App Store. Then download and install the app.

STEP 2: RUN THE PROGRAM

Then launch the app on your computer or iPad.

STEP 3: CONNECT TO WI-FI

Presto also has a feature called Magic Queue, which can store print jobs until you reconnect to Wi-Fi. Perfect for situations where you have something to print but are not near your network or printer. To enable this feature, start by launching an app like Notes or an app that has a box with an arrow pointing out of the icon. Tap the icon, select **More** and select **Presto**. If there's something you want to save, tap its box icon in the upper right corner, then tap **Presto**. You will be redirected to a new page with the Presto queue already selected as the default printer. Click **Print** to save your print job.

STEP 4: CHOOSE A PRINTER

Open an app such as Mail, Safari, or Evernote to test the connection between your iPad and your printer. Most apps have the familiar arrows like the forward and answer icons, or a box with an up arrow. Tap the icon and select Print. The command that appears is the default device. If not, tap Select Printer at the top and scan the printer you checked in step 2 with your iPad. Also, the computer must be on to access the printer.

STEP 5: CHOOSE COPIES

Tap the plus and minus arrows to the right of Copies to select the number of copies to print. At least one copy is required, but you can print up to a total of 99 pages at once if you'd like.

STEP 6: PRINT

After selecting the printer and the number of pages you want, click the print button in the upper left corner of the page. Double-click the Home button to bring up the app switcher and select Print Center or the print view that corresponds to the app you're using to cancel print jobs or check the status.

How to print with Google Cloud Print

You can do almost anything with Google. Printing is no exception. You can use Google Cloud Print to print from Google applications such as Chrome browser, Gmail, and Google Docs. Just sign in to your Google account. You can also print other items from Google Cloud Print using third-party apps.

STEP 1: GET A GOOGLE ACCOUNT

If you made it this far without creating a Google account, you'll have to get one now. Open your Safari browser, and search for Google. Click "**Sign up**" to create you Google account now. You'll be guided through series of steps on the screen to create your profile. Follow the on-screen directions. Fill in all the details asked.

STEP 2: DOWNLOAD PRINTCENTRAL PRO APP

Cloud Print only works with certain Google apps. iPadOS doesn't have inbuilt Google Cloud Print app. You can use PrintCentral Pro instead. Luckily, the app is available from the App Store for $6. After downloading the app, open it.

STEP 3: CHOOSE WHAT YOU WANT TO PRINT

Click on the menu icon (resembles 3 horizontal lines stacked on each other). It's in the top left of the PrintCentral app. After opening the menu, select the file, image, email, document, or web page you want to print. Note that before you print your email, you'll need to make sure your email account is synced with the app. For certain files, make sure those files are added to iCloud first. To print photos, Google simply needs to request access to them and approve the request. Select the print icon. It's found at the top-right edge of the screen.

STEP 4: ADD THE PRINTERS

From there, the Printers (WiFi) page will appear on your device's screen. You can choose to add a printer by clicking the **Add** icon in the upper left corner. Then select **Google Cloud Printing**, enter your Gmail email address, and tap the blue **Save** button.

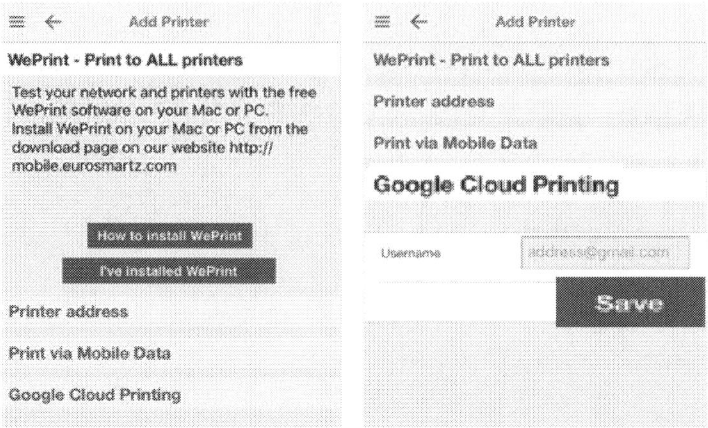

Fig 86. Select Google Cloud Printing, enter your Gmail email address, and tap the blue Save button.

STEP 5: PRINT

Everything should go smoothly from there. Google Cloud Printing selects the correct file and displays the preview page on your device. The file or document you are trying to print appears at the top of your screen. The screen also displays two options. You can either **save it to Google Drive** or change your printer settings. At the bottom of the page are options to **preview**, **print**, or **print later** to organize your print request.

CHAPTER 20: THE IPAD CALENDAR APP

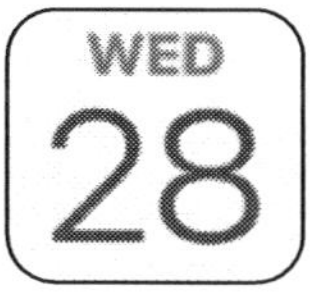

Step-by-step instructions on how to use the calendar app for seniors!

Although many people, even the elderly, appreciate having a pocket diary to keep track of their appointments, but more and more people are switching to digital diaries. Several Apps, including your very own iPad Calendar, which is designed to look and function, like a traditional calendar, are making the transition fairly intuitive. Plus, since iPads are often with us, they are the perfect tool for active seniors who need to keep up with busy schedules on the go. Track doctor appointments, plans with friends, and visits with family all in one place.

Below, we'll show you exactly how to use the iPad Calendar app to create events, view upcoming schedules, and set reminders for important events.

Download the iPad Calendar App

Normally, the iPad Calendar app comes preloaded on iPads. It's usually located in the home screen.

The date will be displayed and will look like the image below.

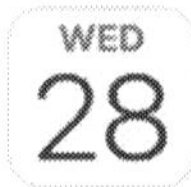

If it gets deleted for some reason, don't worry. You can go to the App Store and reinstall it on your iPad. The method is as follows:

- Tap the icon (App store) in your iPad's home screen.
- Click on the **Search** tab at the bottom of the iPad's screen.
- Type "**Calendar**" in the search bar
- Scroll down until you see the calendar icon and click on '**Get**'. (If it's already installed on your iPad, it will say "**Open**". Tap it to open the app on your iPad.)
- Remember: There are many calendar apps available in the App Store. Be sure to download the Calendar app for iPad. It should be made of a white icon like the one above with red letters and black numbers.

iPad Calendar App Views and Icons

One of the great things about the iPad Calendar app is the 5 different views that the app can display: List, Day, Week, Month and Year.

Whether you want to look one month ahead or one week ahead, you can easily switch views.
Consider it like zooming in and out using different calendar views. You can zoom in to see the entire year and zoom in on a day to see what your schedule looks like. Let's get closer to the end!
To open the iPad Calendar app, click on the Calendar app icon in your home screen.

List View

When it'll be handy: To display a consolidated list of events and appointments.

- Always start by tapping the iPad Calendar icon on the home screen to view the various calendar views.
- Click on the list icon found at the up of the left column. It's made of 3 points and 3 lines in a rectangle.
- This is the List View. You can easily see what you have for the day.

Day View

When it'll be handy: Perfect for viewing the schedule for your day.

- Always start by tapping the iPad Calendar icon on the home screen to view the various calendar views.
- Click on **Day** at the top.

- You've landed in Daily view. You can check the agenda for the day hourly.
- Tap any of the Days of the week at the top to switch to that date.

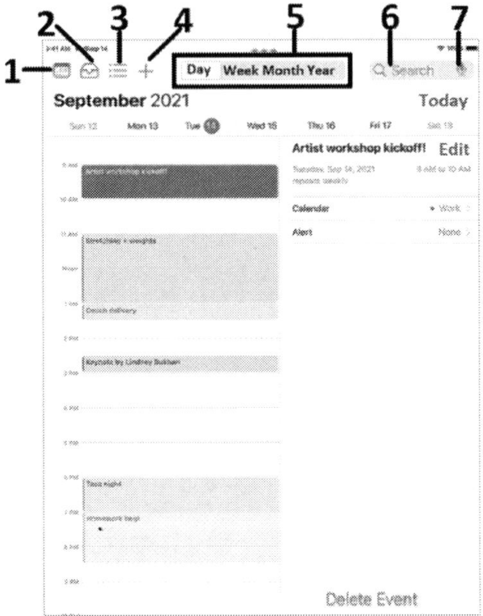

Fig 87- Calendar Day View

1. *Switch Calendars & Accounts*
2. *Check Invitations*
3. *Open List View*
4. *Add Event*
5. *Change between Day, Week, Month & Year Views*
6. *Search box*
7. *Use Voice to search*

Weekly view

When it'll be handy: Look at your week to see if you're free or busy.

To get the most out of the week view, your iPad should be turned sideways (horizontal). To do this, you'll need to open Control Center and make sure portrait orientation lock is turned off.

To open Control Center, swipe down from the upper right side of the screen. (If you also have an iPad with home button, swipe up from the bottom edge of the screen.)

Tap the lock button surrounded by arrows. After tapping, confirm that "Portrait orientation lock: OFF" is displayed.

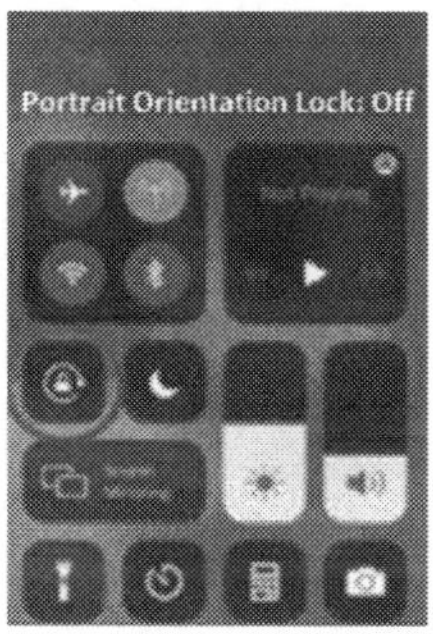

Fig 88- Portrait orientation lock: OFF

Once you're done, close the Control Center by swiping up from the bottom edge of your iPad's screen.

You are now ready for your weekly view. First, tap the Calendar icon 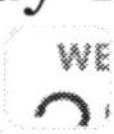 on your iPad's home screen.

Click on **Week** at the top.

Turn your iPad to the horizontal orientation. This will rotate the calendar horizontally, allowing you to view the whole week. You can also swipe down/right to see the next week or swipe up/left to see the previous week.

Monthly view

When it'll be handy: To see what your next holiday is and what you have planned for the month.

First, tap the Calendar icon  on your iPad's home screen.
Click on **Month** at the top.
Swipe Up/Down to switch to other Months.
Next click the icon for List view. You can find it at the up of the calendar display.
A gray dot on a day means there is an event to see on that day of that month. Note that some are for pre-loaded holidays.
Tap any day to view the list of events.

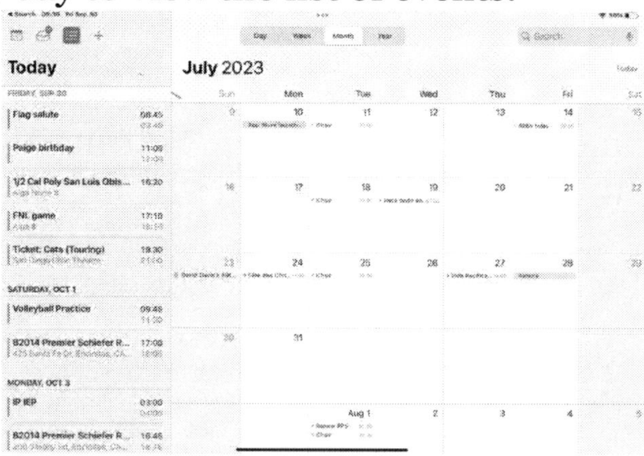

Fig 89- Calendar Month View

Year view

When it'll be handy: Navigate the month quickly. You can easily find out what day of the week Christmas and anniversaries are this year!
The application allows you to scroll up and down to see past or future years. The year view is displayed when you first open the calendar app.
FYI: The calendar app on your iPad already has major US holidays and dates, so if you want to know when the next holiday is, check your iPad calendar.

How to create an event

- Open the Calendar app on your iPad and tap the red plus icon + in the upper left.
- Tap the top box and enter the event title. It can be meetings, appointments, conferences, events, etc.
- Optionally, click **Location/Video Call** and enter a location. You could click FaceTime and then fill in a FaceTime video link if you're planning a remote event. Then click **Start** to set the start time.
- Enter the start time using the numbers on your keyboard.
- If you want to include an end time, scroll down and click on **Ends**. Enter the end time using the keyboard.
- Finally, tap **Add**.
- The event will appear in your calendar.

Add Alert to an event

- Open the calendar app.
- In the Calendar app, tap the event you want to edit.
- Tap "**Edit**" in the upper right corner.
- Scroll down and click on **Alert**.
- Here you can define when the application will remind you of upcoming events. This means that your iPad will ring to remind you of upcoming events.

From here you can also change the event time, title, location and alert time. Then click **Done**. You'll find it at the upper right end of the calendar.

How to delete an event

- First, tap the Calendar icon 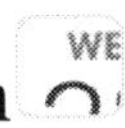 on your iPad's home screen.
- Click on **Day** at the top.
- Tap the event you want to delete in the Calendar app.
- Tap **Delete event**.

How to search for events

- Click the search box (little magnifying glass  that can be found at the top of the calendar display).

- Enter the title in the search bar to search for events by title.
- All past and present dates related to the searched word will be displayed.
- Tap an event to view or edit details.

How to create an event using Siri

If you want to save time and skip typing, Siri can schedule appointments in your calendar by voice. It's like having your own personal assistant!
Press the side button and hold it. This is going to switch on Siri. Or you can just say "Hey, Siri." Colorful bubbles appear at the bottom of the iPad screen. This means Siri is listening for your instruction.

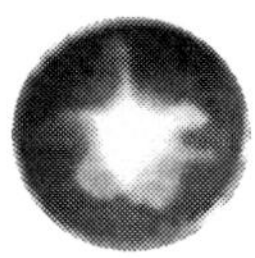

Say, "Schedule an event with William tomorrow at 7:00am." (Insert your own event, location, date and time here!), and Siri will schedule it for you.
Then you have to say "**Confirm**" or click "**Confirm**" to add it to your plan.

CHAPTER 21: CALENDAR SETTINGS

The Calendar app built into iPhone and iPad is not only Apple's personalized event tracker, it's also a gateway to many other productivity apps that sync with it and provide useful information for your daily life. . Even if you use other calendar services like Google or Microsoft, you can connect those services to your Calendar app to get the most out of your daily schedule. Apple's Calendar app has many special customizations that you can use to make it easier to use.

Adjust the Time Zone for Your Calendar Alerts

By default, the iPhone and iPad Calendar apps automatically change time zones when you move between countries. However, there may be times when you want your calendar information to remain in the time zone where you live or work. If you want to change the default timezone, you can override it in your calendar settings.

- Open your device's Settings app
- Scroll down and tap **Calendar**.
- Click **Time Zone Override**.
- Switch on the toggle for Time Zone Override to green.
- Click **Time Zone**.

- Search for the city you want to adjust the timezone to.
- Tap that city to change the default time zone for the calendar app.

How to select a different calendar type

You can change your default calendar type to the Chinese, Islamic, or Hebrew if you follow these.

- Open your device's Settings app
- Scroll down and tap **Calendar**.
- Click **Alternate Calendars**.
- Click **Chinese**, **Hebrew**, or **Islamic**.

How to switch on/off week numbers

By default, the calendar app gives each week of the year a number. For some, this is a convenient way to quickly see how many weeks have passed, but for others it's unnecessary information. This feature can be activated or disabled as required.

- Open your device's Settings app
- Scroll down and tap **Calendar**.
- Click **Week Numbers** and switch on/off the toggle.

How to enable or disable Invitee Declines

If you're good at inviting people to events, you might want to know everyone who has accepted or declined an invitation. However, you may not care who is not at your event. This feature can be activated or disabled as required.

- Open your device's Settings app
- Scroll down and tap **Calendar**.
- Switch on/off the toggle for **Show Invitee Declines**.

How to manage calendar sync

To minimize data usage and internal storage, iPhones and iPads only sync for one month by default. If you're likely to find out-of-date information about events from different calendars, you can change the period for which your accounts are synced.

- Open your device's Settings app
- Scroll down and tap **Calendar**.
- Tap **Sync**.
- Tap the **timeframe** (1 Month, 3 Months, 6 Months, etc.) you want to resync.

Setting the default alert time

You can specify when you want to be notified of calendar events. Events with manually selected notification times are not overridden. This default time is used for alerts for **Birthdays**, **timed events**, & **all-day events**.

- Open your device's Settings app
- Scroll down and tap **Calendar**.
- Click **Default Alert Times**.
- Choose the **Alert** you'll like to set default time for.
- Choose the **Time** you'll like to receive the notice.

Setting a reminder to leave early

You can also enable the option to receive alerts telling you what time you need to leave to reach your event, based on typical travel times for the event your address is at.

- Open your device's Settings app
- Scroll down and tap **Calendar**.
- Click **Default Alert Times**.
- Switch on the toggle for **Time to Leave**.

Changing the Beginning Day of the Week

In the United States, the standard calendar starts on Sunday, which may not work for you. Due to your job, you might think of Monday as the start of the week. If you work a schedule other than 9-5/M-F, you could think of Saturday as first day. You can choose the start date of the week in the Calendar app.

- Open your device's Settings app
- Scroll down and tap **Calendar**.
- Click **Start Week On**.
- Click on a **day of the week**.

How to set the default calendar

You may be trying to keep several Calendars from work, home and other activities. One of them will always be the main calendar. This is typically for creating events. You can set one specific calendar as the default. This means that events are automatically created and shared from that particular account, unless you manually switch to another account.

- Open your device's Settings app
- Scroll down and tap **Calendar**.
- Click **Default Calendar**.
- Choose one calendar that's going to serve as the default calendar of your account.

How to turn location suggestions on or off

When you create an event, the Calendar app includes functionality to suggest a location based on the name you provide. For example, if you plan to have lunch with someone at Applebees, the Calendar app will prompt you to add Applebees location closest to the event. This is going to be handy if you wish to receive an alert when it gets to time to leave for you lunch. This feature can be activated or disabled as required.

- Open your device's Settings app
- Scroll down and tap **Calendar**.
- Turn the location suggestions switch on or off.

CHAPTER 22: HOW TO SET REMINDERS ON IPAD

We're all busy. So it's quite understandable that we sometimes forget activities we're supposed to do. For some of us, it's rather too much, especially when these things are very important. The Reminders app will prove to be a really helpful tool for you to never forget those things you really need to do.

The Reminders app lets you set time and place alerts for important events. The Reminders app lets you create and schedule reminders to keep track of events, daily tasks, shopping lists, tasks, or whatever else you want to keep track of.

Plus, create subtasks within reminders; add attachments, mark important reminders, create reminders based on time and location, select reminders while messaging someone.

Setting up reminders on iPhone and iPad is very easy and you'll get used to it once you create your first reminder on iPad using the following steps.

To open the reminders app, click on the Reminders app icon on the home screen.

Make a Fresh List

- Open your iPad's Reminders app.
- In the Reminders app, press **Add List**.

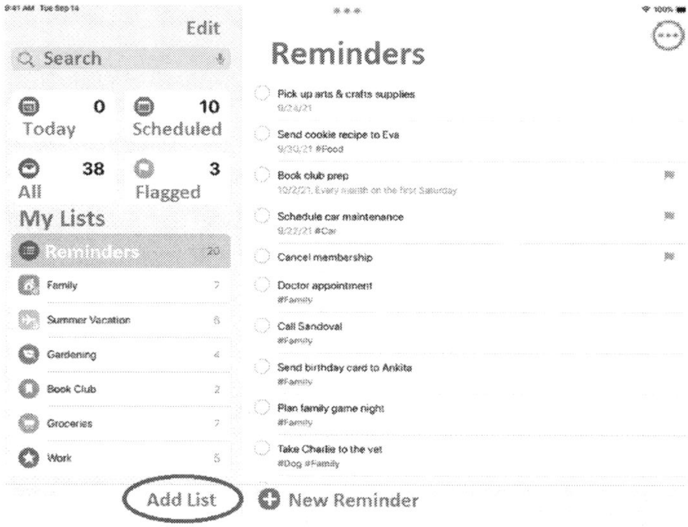

Fig 90- Reminder app interface: Press Add List.

- Pick an account (if you have several).
- Type a name for that list.
- Pick a color for your list.
- Pick a symbol for your list.

Create a new reminder

- Open your iPad's Reminders app 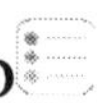.
- On the bottom of the iPad, tap **New Reminder**.
- On the new reminder screen, enter what you want to be reminded about.
- The buttons on top of the keyboard can be used for:

➢ Scheduling Dates and Time:
  - Press 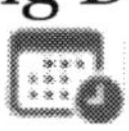

  - Now pick a time and date you'll like to be reminded.
- Add Location:
  - Press
  - Now pick a location where you're going to be reminded (e.g. once you get home or maybe when you enter any Car that has a Bluetooth connection with your iPad).
  - For you to get the location-based reminders, you'll have to do this:
  - ✓ Swipe up to go to your devices Home screen.
  - ✓ Tap Settings
  - ✓ Press Privacy
  - ✓ Click Location Services
  - ✓ Switch on the Location Services (green)
  - ✓ Press Reminders.
  - ✓ Click While Using App
  - ✓ Switch on Precise Location.
- Assign reminder to a person (if the list is a shared list)
  - Press
  - Pick someone from the list (yourself included)
- Flag important reminders: Press
- Attach Photos or documents:
  - Press
  - Do one of these:
  - ✓ Take a fresh picture

   - ✓ Select one of your existing photos
   - ✓ Scan documents

- ➢ Attach scanned text:
   - o Press 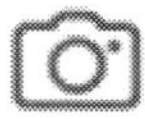
   - o Press Scan Text
   - o Place your device such that the desired text is inside the camera's frame.

- Tap the more icon 
- On the details screen, do these:
   - o Add notes: Press the Notes box. Fill in extra info on that reminder.
   - o Add links to websites: Press the URL box. Fill in a website's address. The reminders app will display a link to that website.
   - o Receive reminders while you chat with a friend in Messages: Switch on (green) **When Messaging.** Pick any of your Contacts from the list. The reminders app will send you a reminder when next you're chatting with that person.
   - o Set Priority tasks: Press **Priority**. Pick **Low**, **Medium** or **High**.
   - o Take your reminder from the present list to a new one: Press List. Then pick one of the lists.
- Press **Done** to save this reminder to your iPad.

Create Subtasks

- Open your iPad's Reminders app.
- Do one of these
    - Press a reminder on the right, swipe your reminder to the right side, and finally press **Indent**
    - Pull one of the reminders onto a second reminder.
    - Once you complete the main task, all it's subtasks are also completed.

Mark Reminders as Completed

- Open your iPad's Reminders app.
- Beside each reminder, you'll find an open circle.
- If you've completed your reminder, press that circle. It will be marked as completed and hidden.
- If you don't want reminders you've completed to be hidden, press more and then press **Show Completed.**
- If you want to delete the reminders you've completed, press more and then press **Clear**

Delete Reminders

You can delete reminders by following these steps:

- Open your iPad's Reminders app.
    - Press a reminder on the right, swipe your reminder to the right side, and finally press **Delete.**

- o If you've gotten an Apple Pencil, simply scribble on the reminder. This will remove the reminder from your iPad immediately.
- o If after deleting a reminder, you immediately change your mind, you can recover it. Immediately press with three of your fingers on the screen. Or shake the iPad.

Modify or Change Existing Reminders

You can change multiple reminders on your iPad by following these steps:

- Open your iPad's Reminders app.
- Press one of your Lists.
- While you're looking at that list, press more
- Press Select Reminders
- Pick the reminders you'll be editing.
- Alternatively, while you're looking at the list, pull over the reminders you'll be editing.
- Use the buttons you find at the bottom of your iPad to do any of these:

➢ Scheduling Dates and Time: Press
Now pick a time and date you'll like to be reminded.

➢ Complete Reminders

➢ Flag important reminders: Press

➢ Assign reminder to a person (if the list is a shared list)

    - Press
    - Pick someone from the list (yourself included)
- Delete Reminders

Keyboard Reminders Shortcuts

If you've gotten an external keyboard, you can use keyboard shortcuts to increase you efficiency while using the Reminders app. Do this:
Connect your keyboard to the iPad.
Use any of these Reminders app Shortcuts:

- Create New Reminder: **Command + N**
- Display Completed Reminders: **Shift + Command + H**
- Display all the reminders that you're assigned: **Command + 5**
- Display extra keyboard shortcuts: Press either the Globe key or the Command key and keep holding till they appear.

CHAPTER 23: HOW TO USE THE NOTES APP

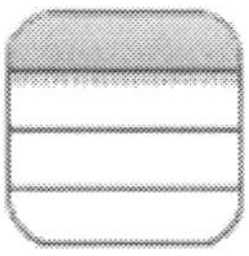

You can easily create and update your notes when you need them. It's as easy as moving it to the Trash when you're done.

There are many times in our daily lives that we have to write something. Whether it's a great idea you have now, an important one to see later or you just want to comment, the Note app in is here for you. Thanks to iOS and iPadOS, it is integrated into your favorite iPhone and iPad, so you do not even need to download another application. And if you use iCloud, everything is synced and accessible from anywhere, even your MacBook.

Let's describe how you can create notes on your iPhone and iPad, and how to edit, move, delete, and restore those notes.

First open Notes. To do it, take these steps:

- Swipe up to return to your device's home screen
- Open the Note app 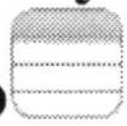 from the home screen of your lovely iPhone or iPad (simply click on it).

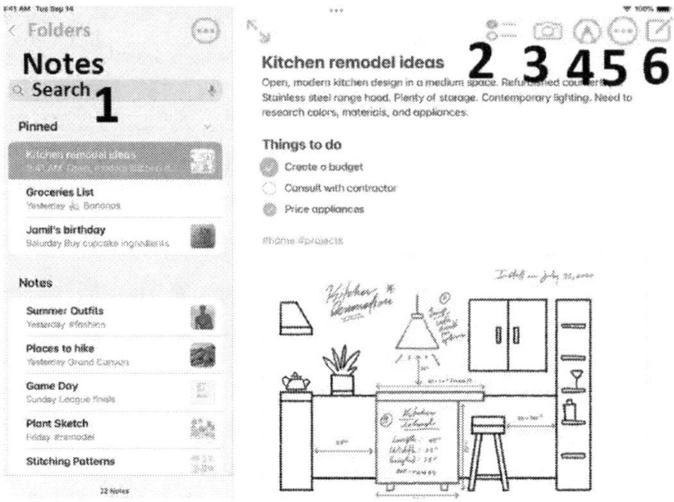

Fig 91- Notes app interface

1. *Search for notes*
2. *Add Checklist to a Note*
3. *Add picture*
4. *Draw or handwrite*
5. *More*
6. *Create a new Note*

How to create a new note on your iPhone or iPad

- Swipe up to return to your device's home screen
- Open the Note app 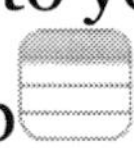 from the home screen of your lovely iPhone or iPad (simply click on it).
- Click the Create New Notes key 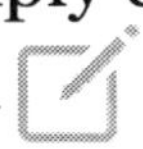 at the top.
- Type your Note.

- The first line of your Note will serve as the Title, so type something direct but meaningful here.
- Press Aa and format your write up (for example add heading style, make fonts bold or italics, make a bulleted list, make a numbered list, make a table, etc.)
- Click the Done button to save the note and exit edit mode.
- Click the New Note button on the top of the current note to quickly start another note.

Funky-Tip: You can set a Standard Style that'll be used for all the first lines of your fresh notes. Do this:

- Open Settings app
- Press **Notes**
- Press the option for what **New Notes** are going to **Start With**.

Another Funky-Tip: If your iPad goes into Lock Screen mode, and an idea comes, you can quickly make a note or continue from the last note you were making. You simply have to modify how your Lock Screen behaves. Do this:

- Open Settings app
- Press **Notes**
- Press the option for **Access Notes** when you're in **Lock Screen**.

How to modify an existing note on your iPhone or iPad

1. Open the notes app from the home screen of your iPhone or iPad
2. Press a note you'll be modifying.
3. Press anywhere in the note to display the keypad and open Update or Add.
4. Make your changes.
5. Click **Done** to save what you've changed.

Add Checklist to a Note

1. Open the notes app from the home screen of your iPhone or iPad
2. Press a note you'll be modifying.
3. Press at the top.
4. Do one of these:
    - Add items to your list: Type text in. Then press **return** in your keyboard. Type in the next item, press return and continue the cycle till your list is complete.
    - Enlarge or diminish the indentation for your list: Swipe to the left/right on any of the list items.
    - Mark one of the items in your list as completed: Press the empty circle close to that item. A checkmark in the circle means complete.

- Reorder items: Press the empty circle or checked one, hold it and push that item to the new location.
- Manage the items in your list: Press the list, when the menu comes up, press. Now press Checklist. Press one of these:
    - Check All.
    - Uncheck All.
    - Delete Checked.
    - Move Check Bottom.

Funky-Tip: You can configure your iPad to sort items you've checked to the bottom of your notes automatically. Do this:

- Open Settings app
- Press **Notes**
- Press **Sort Checked Items**
- Press **Automatically**

Insert Tables

1. Open the notes app from the home screen of your iPhone or iPad
2. Press .
3. Do one of these:
4. Fill in texts: Press a cell and then type in the text. If you want to enter a new line within that cell, press the Shift key and hold it. Press next.

5. Move over to the next cell: Press next. After getting to the ending cell, press next to begin a fresh row.
6. Format rows or columns: Press the selection handle for that row or column. Then press a style (bold, underline, strikethrough or italic).
7. Add/delete rows or columns: Press the selection handle for that row or column. Press Add or Delete.
8. Move rows or columns: Press the selection handle for that row or column. Push it to the location.
9. Show more columns: When your table gets wider than your iPad's screen, swipe the table to the right or left to show the other columns.

Funky-tip: You can remove the table you've created and then change the contents of that table to text. Super Easy! Press one of the cells in your table. Press and then press **Convert to Text**.

Keyboard Shortcuts for Notes app

If you've gotten an external keyboard, you can use keyboard shortcuts to increase you efficiency while using the Notes app. Do this:

Connect your keyboard to the iPad.

Use any of these Notes app Shortcuts:

- Create new note: Command + N
- Add Checklist: Shift + Command + L
- Hide Sidebar: Control + Command + S

- Display extra keyboard shortcuts: Press either the Globe key or the Command key and keep holding till they appear.

How to delete notes on iPhone or iPad

1. Open the notes app from the home screen of your iPhone or iPad
2. Press a note you'll be modifying.
3. Click the More button (three dots) in the top right corner.
4. Click **Delete**.
5. To quickly delete a note, swipe left on the note in the list, and then tap **delete**.
6. This will send that note to the "Recently deleted" folder for 30 days, after which the temporarily deleted note comment will be permanently deleted.

CHAPTER 24: HANDWRITING WITH APPLE SCRIBBLE

You can use the scribble function to enter handwritten text on your iPad. If you have an Apple Pen, bring it close by, because it's going to be an handy tool. If you don't, there's no problem. You can use your fingers instead.

Handwritten on iPad!

Ever wanted to use handwriting on a note, picture, message or something else with your iPad? Thanks to Apple Scribble, it's now possible. Ideal for writing notes or practically any other thing your amazing mind can imagine writing or drawing. Scribble converts it to text. You can use it to fill in text fields, set reminders, write comments and more. Good news for those who do not want to fiddle the on-screen keyboard.

Scribble has many features you need to learn to enhance the experience, such as designing specific patterns to perform various functions (for example, zigzag for deleting).

If you've gotten an Apple Pencil, Wonderful!

This chapter describes the basic and advanced features of Scribble to help you get the most out of Scribble.

How to enter handwritten text using Scribble

➢ Set up "**Try Scribble**"

- Swipe up to return to your device's home screen.
- Open Settings app 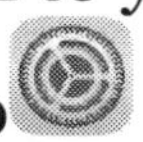
- Scroll through and press **Apple Pencil**
- Next, press **Try Scribble**. A Handwriting tab pops-up. Start writing in the tab and you can write larger text outside this tab as well.

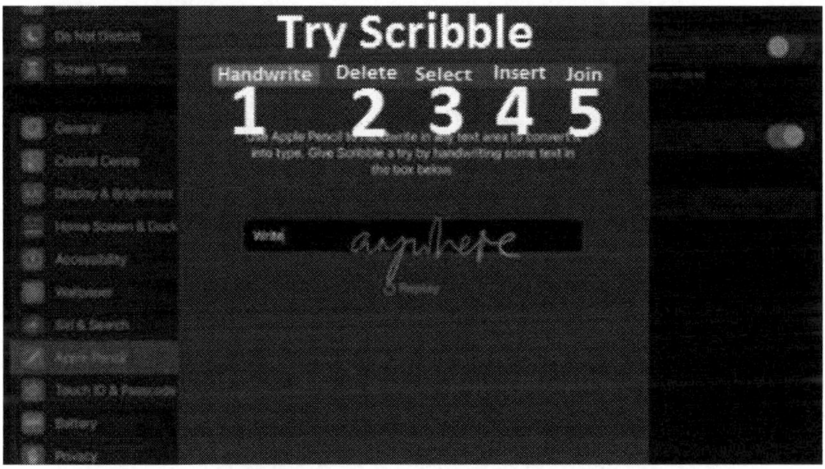

Fig 92- Try Scribble

1. Handwrite
2. Delete
3. Select
4. Insert
5. Join

➢ Draw a zigzag across your word for deletion. A vertical or horizontal zigzag works well.

Or Press the **Delete** tab to see how the word is deleted when you press it.
After a few taps, the iPadOS will start working, but you can continue with your writing.

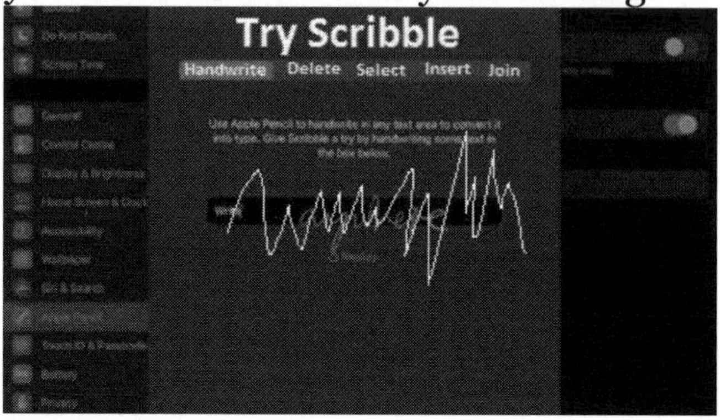

Fig 93- Draw a zigzag across your word

- Select text

Press **Select**.
Try drawing a solid horizontal line in the text or drawing a circle around the text to select the text. Again, Scribble selects the entire word, but you can drag the blue handle to add or remove letters.

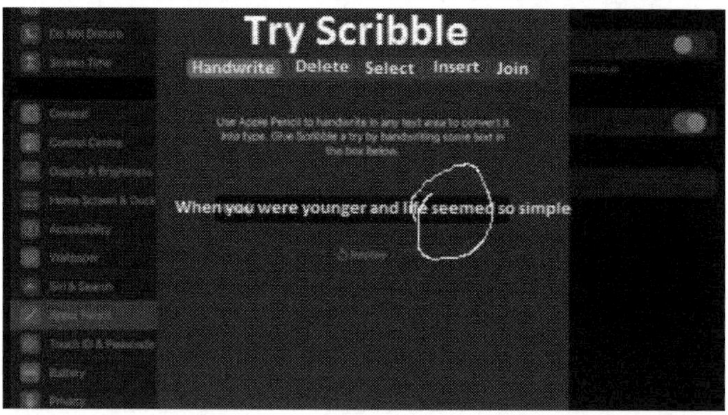

Fig 94- Drawing a circle around the text

- Enter text

Press **Insert**.
The Insert tab shows how to press and hold to enter text, but it is not necessary. Just press to enter the cursor, type text and enter.

- Join text

Press Join
Draw vertical lines to add or remove spaces, as shown in Join.

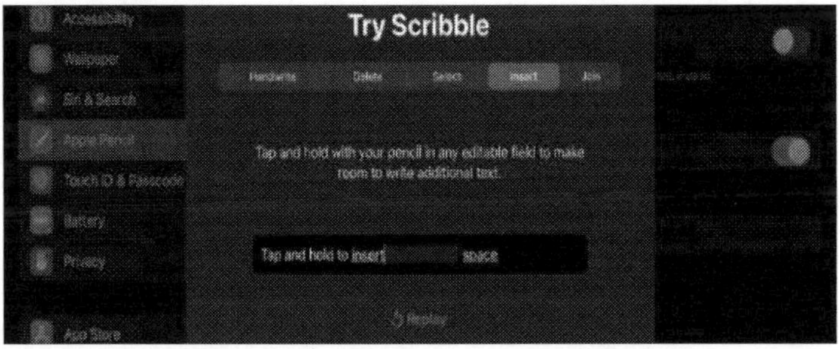

Scribble can be used anytime, anywhere
Scribble will not need to "learn" how you write. It works with standard text input fields. To illustrate, when you're browsing in Safari, you can write in the search field and click on one of the suggestions. You can also write directly in the text box on the web page.

Scribble text within apps

Scribble also works with text boxes in your apps (you may need to click the box first).

Handwriting on iPad: How to use the advanced features of Scribble in Notes

Press Markup Pen

- Open the notes app
- Press a note you'll be modifying.

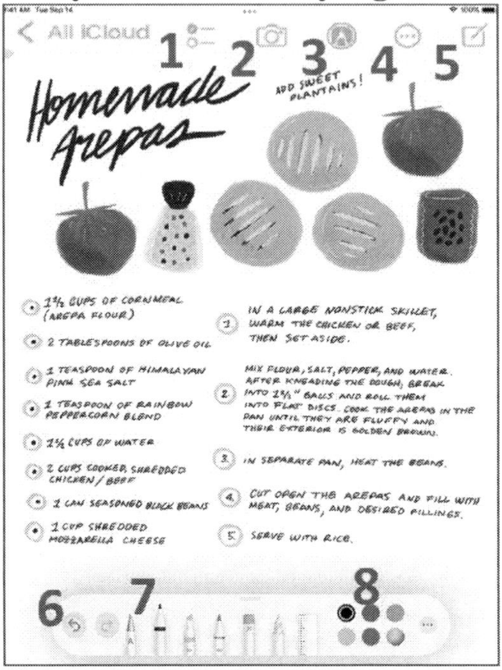

1. Create Checklist
2. Add images
3. Mark Up Tool (Handwrite/draw) New Note
4. Right back tool (new line)
5. Different writing tools
6. Colors

- On Note Application in iPadOS, you can use Scribble in two ways (this may vary depending on the application to receive feedback from third parties).

- On the note, tap the markup icon in the upper right corner and select a new writing pen ('A').
- Use an Apple Pen to write anywhere on the note screen to see the recognized characters entered in the current cursor. Notice the Back Right button. Press this button to start a new line.
- Or Draw with your finger
- Select another pen tool to write text of any size you want. This works without a pencil. Click the three-dot icon on the Markup bar at the bottom and activate the 'Draw with your finger'.

Select the text

Remove the marker pen at the top and use your finger to press and hold until the text you wrote is highlighted. Drag the yellow selection handles to select more (even multiple rows) or fewer. Press to change options.

Edit and search

You can edit and search for handwritten text. (If this is the first line, the title of the note will be set as well.) You can select Copy as text to add it as plain text to the iPadOS clipboard and paste it elsewhere.

Try Shape Analysis

Shape analysis is also new. With your finger or Apple Pen, draw a rough square, triangle, circle, star or hexagon and keep holding your finger or pen down. Your drawing will pop into a perfect shape which you can move and select.

CHAPTER 25: CAMERA AND VIDEORECORDING

Using the Camera app

Take photos and videos on iPad using the camera app. It is designed to work closely with a Photo app that allows you to view, organize and edit your pictures and videos.

To access the camera from the lock screen:

You can quickly access the camera from the lock screen. Simply swipe left to open the app immediately. You do not need to open the device first.

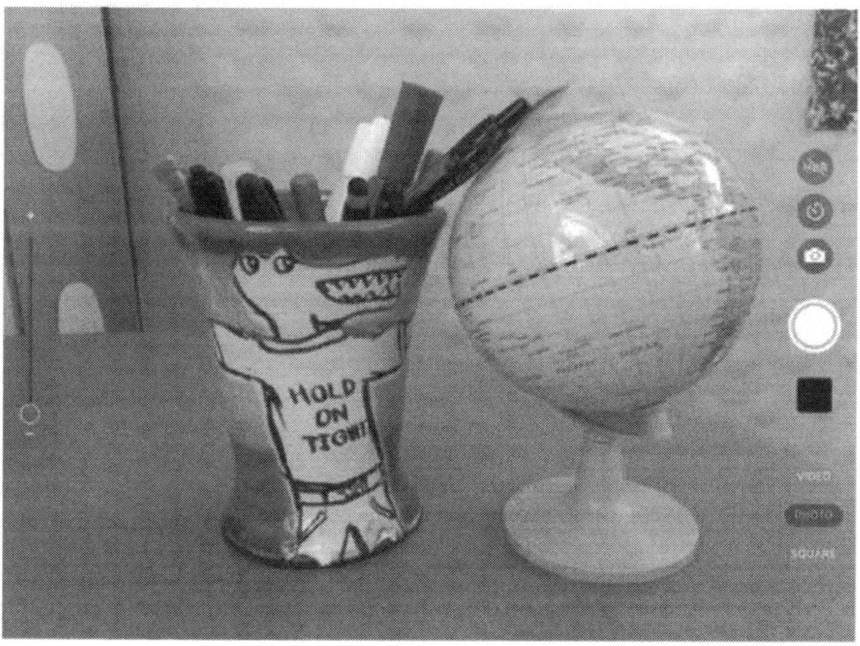

Zoom in and out

When taking a picture, pinch to zoom in and out. However, keep in mind that the iPad uses digital zoom instead of the optical zoom lens (as seen on larger cameras). Digital zoom tries to mimic optical zoom. As a result, zooming leads to poor image quality.

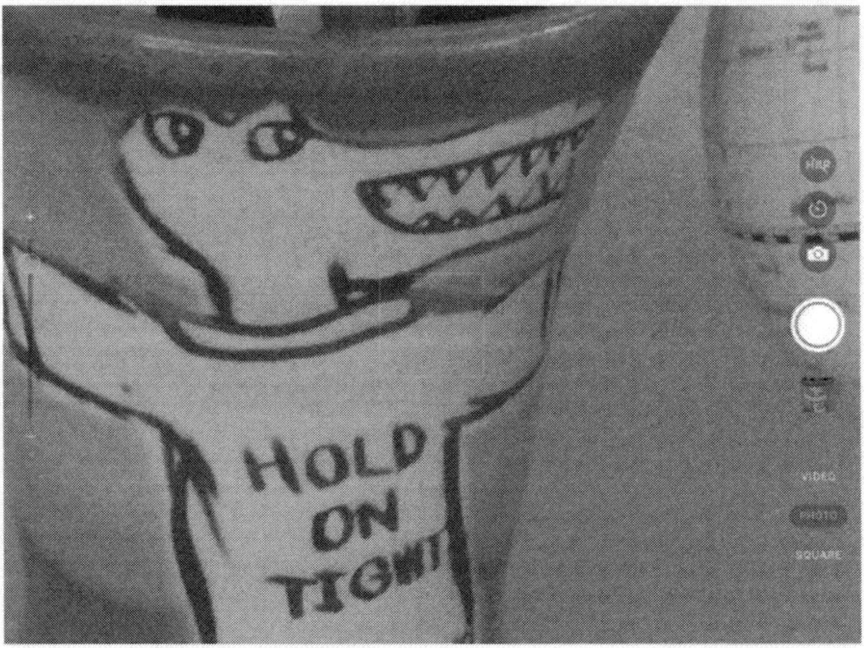

Camera direction

Rotate iPad to change camera orientation from landscape to portrait.

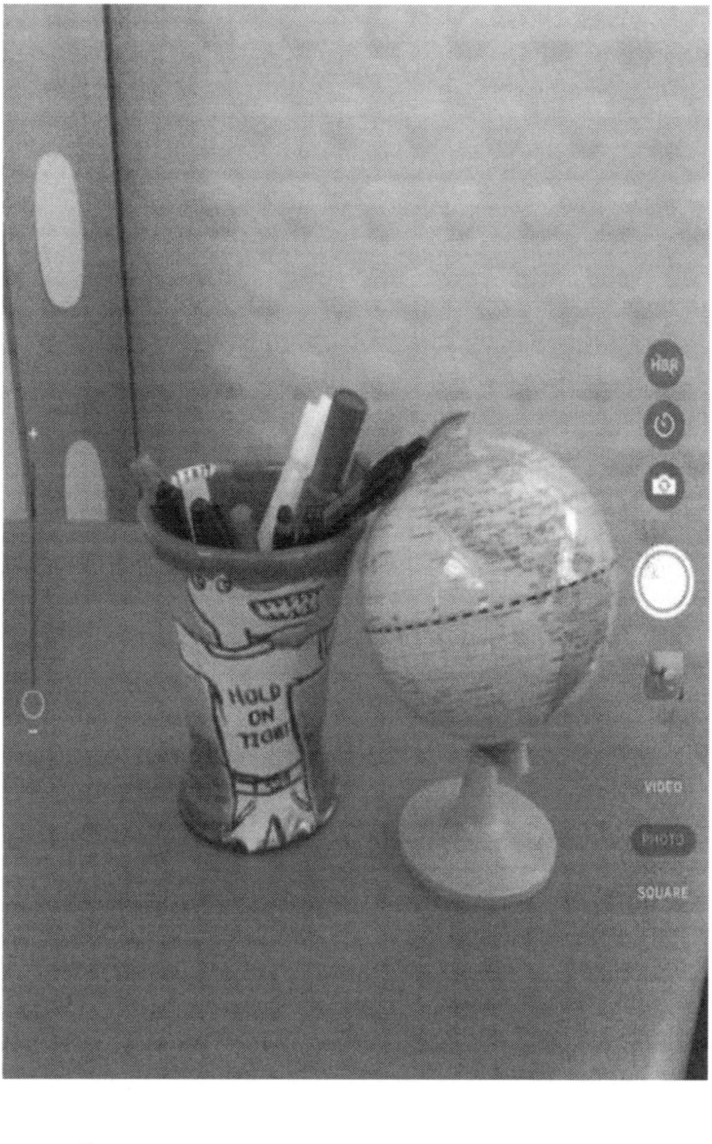

Turn the camera over

Tap the Flip Camera button in the upper right corner to switch between the front and rear cameras. You can take a picture of yourself with the front of the camera. Also use the front camera for video conferencing applications such as FaceTime.

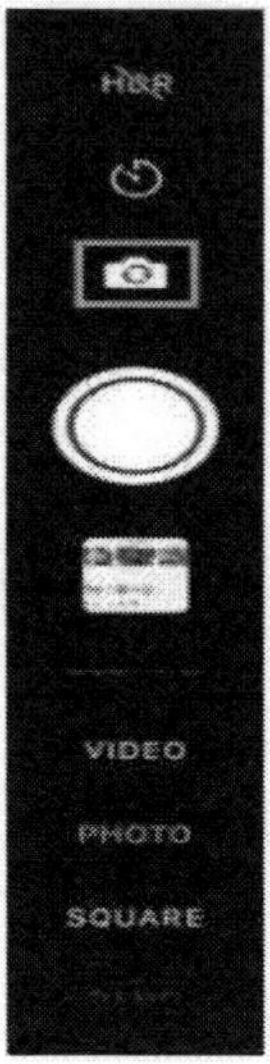

Video recording

You can also record videos with the camera app. To do this, swipe to Video and then tap the Record button.

Take a screenshot

Take a screenshot. At the same time, press and release the buttons at the top, and release one of the volume keys.

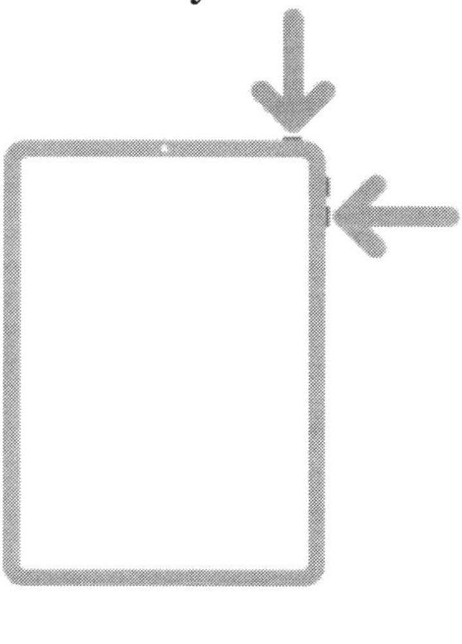

CHAPTER 26: PHOTO

Take a photo or video on your iPad and you get it directly in the Photos app. You can use photos to organize your photos and videos in albums, create slideshows, and share media in a variety of ways.

Image processing

The Photos app also allows you to edit your photos with simple options like rotating, enlarging, removing red-eye and cropping. This is an easy way to fix small image problems without the use of a sophisticated image printer.
To access the options, tap the Edit button while viewing the image in full screen.

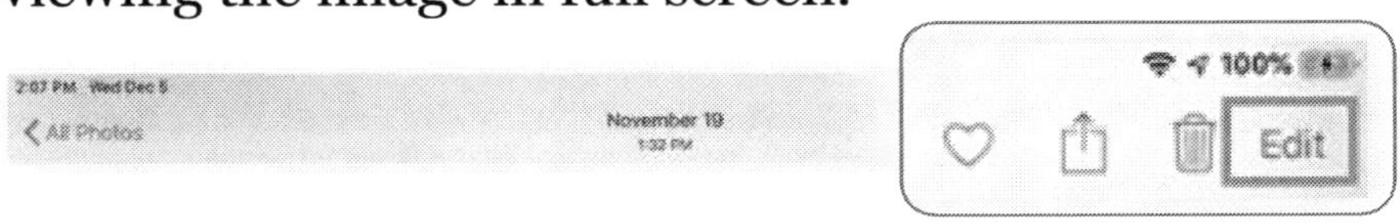

Editing options appear next to the screen. When you have finished editing the image, tap **Done**.

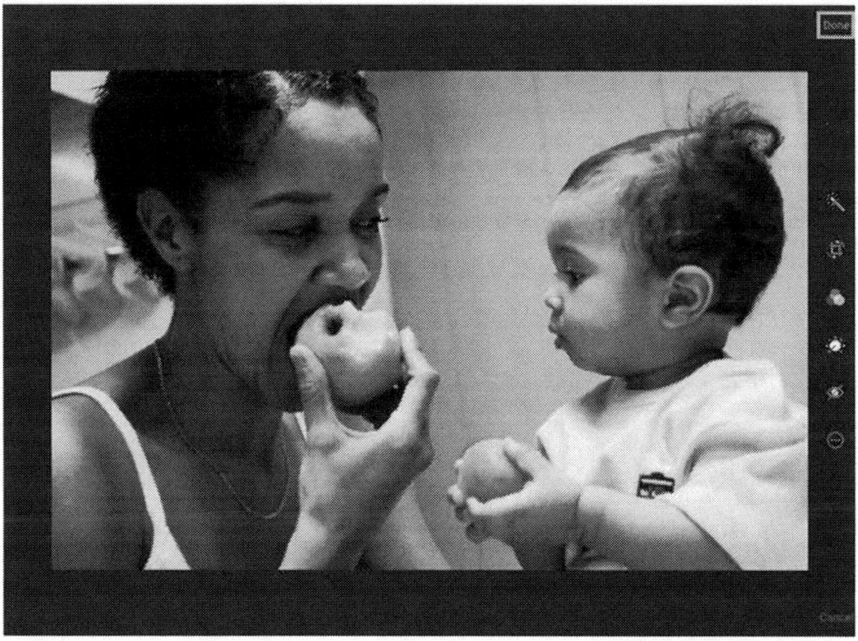

Share Photos

There are many ways to share pictures from your iPad. For example, you can send a photo as an email attachment, post it on Facebook or instagram, or play it in a slideshow on your iPad. Simply tap the Share button in the upper right corner, select the photos you want to share and then select the option you want.

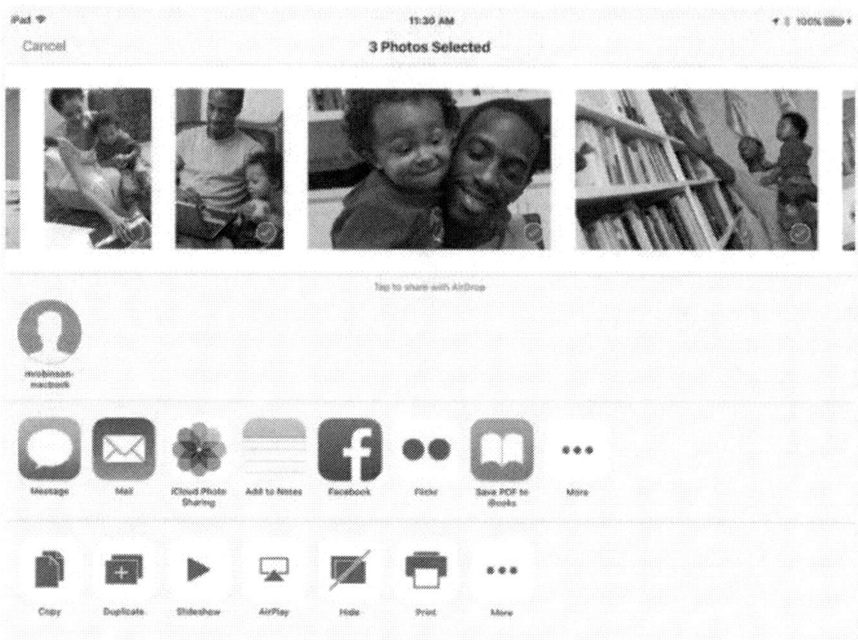

You can transfer photos from your iPad to your computer by connecting your iPad to your computer using the included USB cable.

Method 1: Import to Mac

- You're going to need a USB cable. First, connect your iPad and Mac computer using the USB Cable.

- Open the Photos app on your computer.

- The Photos application will display an import screen containing all the images and videos on the connected device. If the import screen does not appear automatically, click the device name in the image bar.

- When prompted, use your password to unlock your iOS or iPad OS device. If your iOS or iPadOS device asks you to trust this computer, tap Trust to continue.

- Select a location to import your photos. Next to Import, you can select an existing album or create a new one.

- Choose the pictures you wish to import and tap **Import Selected**, or click **Import All New Photos**. Wait until the process is complete before disconnecting the device from your Mac.

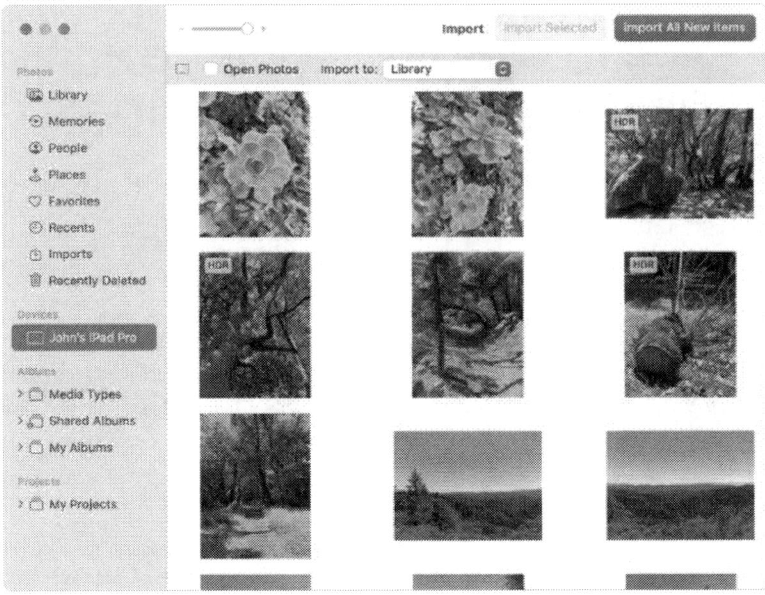

Method 2: How to download photos from iPad to Mac using iPhoto

You can also use iPhoto to download photos from iPad to Mac. Follow the steps below.

Step 1: Connect the USB cable to connect your iPad to your Mac.

Step 2: Open your MacBook's iPhoto. iPhoto shows the photos saved on your iPad.

Step 3: Select the images you want to import. Then click Import Options.

Step 4: When done, you will be asked if you want to delete or keep the images after importing.

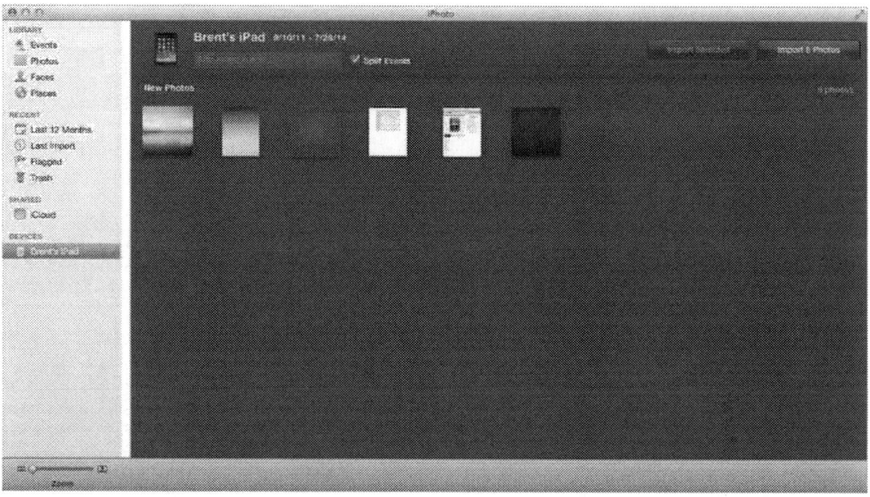

Method 3: How to copy iPad photos to Mac with Image capture

The following steps will show you how to transfer iPad photos to Mac with photo capture.

Step 1: Connect your iPad and Mac computer using the USB Cable.
Step 2: Open the Image Capture app on your Mac.
Step 3: Choose the photos you wish to import to your Mac.

Step 4: Select a location to save your Mac photos. Then click Import or Import All.

Step 5: When you are done, you will see that the imported images have a green check mark.

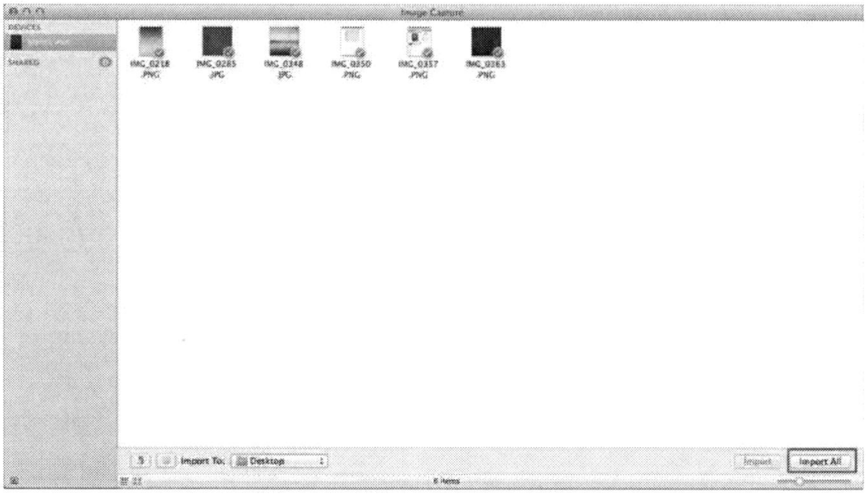

WHAT NEXT

Well Done! You've made it to the end of this big book. Or was it? You probably still need to go over several chapters again for better understanding. And like our readers often say, you never know how little you know about a book, until you need to apply its advice. So don't be quick to discard it. If possible, let it be among your documents. We sincerely apologize if there was anything you just couldn't understand. Please let us know about it in your review and we'll definitely work to improve on that.

It was wonderful having you around and we hope you'll be able to check out our other books. Don't forget to rate this book.

The Publishers,

Funky Traders

Rate this book

If you'll like to rate this book, please visit amazon and leave a positive review.

Other books you may like

Visit the links below to access our other books.
IPHONE 14 USER GUIDE FOR SENIORS & BEGINNERS by Henry K Mills
www.amazon.com/dp/B0BDM9J74B

IPHONE SE USER GUIDE 3 by HENRY K MILLS
www.amazon.com/dp/B09XWXQPD9

IPAD AIR USER GUIDE 5th Generation (2022) by CASTOR TRUMP
https://www.amazon.com/dp/B09Y9862T7

APPLE WATCH SERIES 8 USER GUIDE by Henry K Mills
www.amazon.com/dp/B0BDVWRQX5

MACBOOK AIR USER GUIDE (M2 Chip & M1 Chip)
www.amazon.com/dp/B0B6QPB1RJ

ADOBE PHOTOSHOP CC 2022 BEGINNERS GUIDE by James McCurry
www.amazon.com/dp/B0B7XNQYNW

CANON EOS R7 USER GUIDE by James McCurry
Digital Photography & Videography Manual on Connectivity, Camera Parts, Buttons, Dials, Setting Up, Menus, Shooting Modes, Settings, Video Tips
www.amazon.com/dp/B0BGQGM47V

INDEX

G

H

I

K

L

R

S

Printed in Poland
by Amazon Fulfillment
Poland Sp. z o.o., Wrocław
23 May 2023

ad8f2cd4-71b6-4527-9322-8aad3aaafb05R01